PRAISE FOR

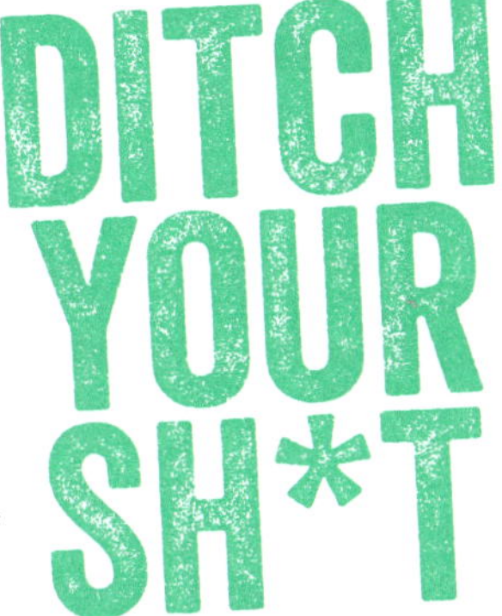

"*Ditch Your Sh*t* feels like your big sister (that's allowed to cuss—a lot!) giving you a tough love pep talk for cleaning your room. Kate Evans breaks down the mental component to why your home is cluttered so you can break through and get your stuff tidied up and organized. Get ready to break through previous barriers and tackle those spots that you haven't figured out yet. Kate's approach blends realistic expectations and practical methods to help you get stuff done."

—**BECKY RAPINCHUK**, 4x author and founder of Clean Mama

"Kate Evans delivers equal inspiration and motivation in *Ditch Your Sh*t*, sharing her personal story, generous wisdom, and plenty of practical checklists that actually inspire action. This isn't another book you'll dog-ear and forget. It's the clutter-clearing companion you'll reach for again and again as you move through your home, one room at a time."

—**AMANDA GIBBY PETERS**, founder of Simple Shui and House Therapy

"What sets this work apart from typical organizing guides is its emphasis on intentionality and joy as organizing principles. This book reframes decluttering as an act of self-care and environmental nurturing rather than punishment or deprivation... This is a resource I would confidently recommend to colleagues for both personal reflection and potential integration into practice."

—**JADA BUTLER**, PA-C, LPC

"Someone in the organizing community once shamed me for calling a client's belongings 'stuff.' A decade later, in a world overflowing with chaos and overwhelm, I'm glad we can finally call out what's really holding us back: the sh*t cluttering our homes, minds, and lives. Kate Evans offers a bold and refreshing approach to decluttering—one rooted not in shame, but in self-care. With equal parts tough love and strategic magic, this book is a must-read for anyone ready to let go of the past and create a future that's fully aligned."

—**MONICA LEED**, CEO & Owner of Simply Spaced and author of *Simply Spaced: Clear the Clutter and Style Your Life*

DITCH YOUR SH*T

DITCH YOUR SH*T

DECLUTTERING YOUR MINDSET TO DECLUTTER YOUR HOME

KATE EVANS

TURNER PUBLISHING COMPANY
Nashville, Tennessee
www.turnerpublishing.com

Cover design by William Ruoto
Book design by Anna Knighton

Library of Congress Control Number: 2024048121

Printed in the United States of America

CONTENTS

FOR SHAWN,

the punk rocker love of my life who believes in me even when he thinks I've lost my mind.

AND AMY,

my lifelong friend and writing coach who put up with my crap and made me a better writer.

INTRODUCTION: SHIT'S ABOUT TO GET REAL

I want you to feel the way I did the day I stood in my tidy, decluttered kitchen and realized: *Decluttering your home is self-care.*

Your home is a reflection of you, and you are a reflection of your home.

When your home is a hot, chaotic mess, so is your brain. Think about the most cluttered place in your home. Does your mind feel like that space? And if your mind is a swirling hell-hole of chaos, your home will be too.

This is the connection between feeling overwhelmed with the state of your home and feeling stuck and unmotivated in your life. No one should feel like they are broken or failing because their home is cluttered or untidy. Insight, skills, and systems are all you need to get it together.

This book teaches you how to declutter your home by decluttering yourself. It gives you simple, easy ways to hack through the mental clutter that leads to physical clutter in the first place, to create the life and home you want.

That's why you bought this book, right? To get all that crap sorted out. To feel better about yourself and your house. This book is going to give you the tools to tackle your home and your life in a way that will make them both better than ever.

WHY DOES CLUTTER KEEP COMING BACK?

Okay, so if decluttering is self-care, what is clutter, anyway?

If your answer is "All the crap I have around my house," or "The stuff piled up that I keep avoiding," you aren't alone. And, technically, you aren't wrong.

Clutter is more than the physical stuff, though. Clutter starts in your head. It's how you think, how you feel, and how you live your life. The stuff all over your house is the scapegoat. It's a symptom of your internal chaos.

If you don't look at yourself first, that physical pileup will never stop happening.

That's why you picked this book up out of the stacks of awesome books on decluttering that are out there. Because you know something has been missing.

A home doesn't clutter itself. It gets that way because the mind of the homeowner is cluttered.

I know people. Without unsticking the mental clutter, the physical clutter has no chance. You can get rid of all your stuff and still be cluttered. You might call it disorganized, but it's really clutter until you've addressed your mental shit.

That's the thing you knew was missing. *You.* Your personality shapes your progress. There is no one-size-fits-all here. You need a customized reassessment of your relationship between yourself and your home. That's why you've tried so many times to get motivated, but it fell by the wayside.

I'm going to explain how people change, and why.

The work I'm going to ask you to do is going to be hard. Introspective, yes. Insightful, yes. And did I mention hard? But what did you ever get in life that was really worth it without a little sweat?

You're going to investigate yourself. Then you'll investigate your home. The reality is that you'll do this over and over in the coming years.

The great part is that you'll put a new puzzle piece in place with each rotation. Over time, with patience and courage, you'll create a whole new life perspective for yourself and evolve your home into what you've always wanted.

HERE'S HOW THIS SHIT'S GOING TO GO

This book isn't just going to teach you about yourself: it's also going to teach you how to figure out what the hell has been holding you back from decluttering your home and what to do about it. After all the useful crap in this chapter about what to expect and who the hell I am, you'll get into the shit you bought this book for.

THE FIRST HALF

The first half is your traditional self-help book: decluttering your mental shit. In this part, you'll get down and dirty with all of the stuff that clogs up your mental and emotional works.

First, we'll talk about readiness.

The reason you haven't done something yet may be as simple as not having been emotionally ready to do it. As you read through the rest of the book, I want you to be able to check in with yourself as to whether you're ready to change something or if you're still thinking about it and need a little more mental work to get you there.

You'll learn about your limiting beliefs, face your fears, poke at your perfectionism, and dismantle your shame.

Why? Because all of that is holding you back. You'll take a look at those shitty messages you've been carrying around with you that say "I'm not good enough," or "I don't deserve to have a home and life I love."

That's all just to warm you up. Next, you'll take a hard look at the things you really value that give you energy so you can build on them. You'll get rid of the crap you think you're supposed to value that's draining your energy, keeping you from getting motivated.

And I know you have some habits that you say are "just the way I am." To which I say, "Bullshit." Habits are learned, so they can be unlearned or replaced by new habits that don't make you feel like you're always chasing your tail. So, you'll take a deep look at those habits of yours and figure out what you'd rather be doing with your time and energy.

I promise a really horrifying story about how big of a slob I once let myself be.

Every good life coach and therapist knows you can't just stir up a bunch of crap in a client and then send them out into the world without something solid to hold on to. You need to build skills and share information that help the client feel like they can take everything they've learned about themself and start applying it.

☆ SUCCESS STRATEGY ☆

When you read something that really hits home in this book, underline it, highlight it, or write it in a journal.

That's why you'll finish up the first half by setting your goals. Not as easy as it sounds! There's a hell of a lot of honesty that has to go into goal-setting. But don't you worry: I'll walk you through it, and you'll be ready to move on to the second part, no problem.

THE SECOND HALF

This is where the rubber meets the road: decluttering your physical shit. As in, "how to apply all of that mental crap I just learned to the heap of physical crap I'm drowning in at home." This is the stuff all of those other decluttering books you've read have touched on but never quite explained. This is where you'll start to understand why reading this book is what will make that pile of other decluttering books—plus the podcasts, blogs, and social media posts you've saved—finally work for you.

In Chapter 7, "Let's Declutter Some Shit!" I'll give you a quick breakdown of basic decluttering skills so you can have them in mind as you face the shit in each area of your home and get excited to take action.

Throughout the rest of Part 2, you're going to apply what you learned in Part 1 to decluttering. You'll tackle the main rooms in your house that need some love one by one, along with a few other categories of clutter that might be shoved into closets and other dark places. At the same time, I'm going to normalize the shit out of your life with stories of others' decluttering journeys.

☆ SUCCESS STRATEGY ☆

Keep those things you highlighted in Part 1 in mind while reading Part 2. It will help make sense of your own home.

Before I help you face your kitchen, the hub of your home, which feels like a constantly moving target, I'll tell you about my breaking point, which happened in my kitchen, and my hallelujah moment, which also happened in my kitchen.

In the chapter tackling the bathroom, you'll be taking a deep, hard look at why under the sink, in your shower, and in your linen closet are all places that are overflowing with crap. I'll even point out some physical stuff that you might still be using that could be harmful because of its age. That's right, this is some serious shit.

There's a ton of space in your home that is used by everyone, and it becomes a magnet for chaos the second you turn your back on it all. Living rooms, entryways, playrooms—you know, those kinds of places. You think your space is a wreck? Let me tell you some stories that start with "Dear God, no" and end with "Ahhhh."

After dealing with shared spaces, you'll be ready to dive into the private space of your bedroom. Feng Shui tells us the bedroom needs to have the least amount of stuff, mental and physical, in it to keep the energy clear for good sleep.

No, I'm not going to give you shit about having a TV in your bedroom—I have one too.

I am going to hit your closet and dressers hard, though, so get ready (I promise to be gentle—maybe).

Once you're sick of thinking about how many of your fears are hiding in your closet, you get to move on to your dirty little secrets—all the places you hide shit, like garages, attics, and sheds. And don't get me started on off-site storage lockers!

Finally, what decluttering book is complete without talking about sentimental clutter? That's all the crap you can get attached to and don't even ask yourself why. You're going to get into the muck and separate the true treasures from the crap that drags you down with guilt and shame.

THE EXTRA HELPFUL BITS

I want you to have some quick-hit info, details to increase your understanding of the topic at hand, and lots of exercises to put your decluttering in action. So, I've put these three things into each chapter:

Success Strategies: Quick tips to spark insight and interest.

Things That Make You Go Hmmm . . . : Explanations of tools and concepts beyond the mental. For example, I show you how to file fold clothes in Chapter 12 ("Well, Shit, Half My Clothes Still Have Tags") to decode the benefits and steps of this particular method.

Making It Real: Guided exercises to help you apply the information in the book to your own life.

AND IN THE END

By the time you get to the end of this book, you'll understand yourself a hell of a lot better, you'll be comfortable welcoming surprise guests who drop by your decluttered house, and you'll have a set of skills that will make you a very dangerous person to any future clutter that tries to emerge in your mind or your home.

THINGS THAT MAKE YOU GO HMMM . . .

We all have teachers, and many of mine have written books and provided great social media, podcasts, and YouTube channels. Here are some of my faves on clearing mental and physical clutter that I think you'll enjoy too.

BOOKS	*Clear Your Clutter with Feng Shui* by Karen Kingston	*Simply Clean* by Becky Rapinchuk	*Simple Shui for Every Day* by Amanda Gibby Peters
	*The Life-Changing Magic of Not Giving a F*ck* by Sarah Knight	*Decluttering at the Speed of Life* by Dana K. White	*Sink Reflections* by Marla Cilley, The FlyLady
	The Gentle Art of Swedish Death Cleaning by Margareta Magnusson	*The Life-Changing Magic of Tidying Up* by Marie Kondo	*Simply Spaced* by Monica Leed
INSTAGRAM	@janettheorganizer	@goodleaflife	@amandagibbypeters
	@cleanmama	@simplyclean	@neatmethod
	@shiragill	@athomewithnikki	@howtogyst
YOUTUBE	How to Get Your Shit Together	Do It on a Dime	The Secret Slob
	Brittany Vasseur	Clutter Bug	Yoga with Kassandra
PODCASTS	*How to UnF*ck Your Brain*	*Got Clutter? Get Organized!*	*Happier with Gretchen Rubin*
	Clearing the Clutter Inside	*Mindful Productivity Podcast*	*Let's Purify!*

WHO THE HELL IS THIS WOMAN WHO THINKS SHE KNOWS SO DAMN MUCH?

I'm a person just like you. A person just like the authors and podcasters and bloggers mentioned before. A person with a particular set of skills to get you the shit you need.

I've been working with the psychology of human beings for over twenty years, and I've never seen a quick fix cure anything.

Trauma, grief, life transitions, bruised egos, divorces, births: I've heard it all as a therapist and life coach. I've seen the worst in human beings, and I've seen the best.

As a yoga teacher, I've seen people quit before they begin. I've seen them push too hard and hurt themselves. I've seen them doubt their ability and not take the risk to try.

It's amazing how similar people are to each other, and yet how alone we can feel. If humans were really all so different from one another, I'd never be able to do my job. So, when clients or students are frustrated at the slowness of the process, I always tell them the same thing:

"Success is not about being perfect or even good at something. It's about the willingness to commit to yourself and be consistent in your work."

I've read books and books and books on decluttering, organizing, and cleaning and have done the trainings offered through the National Association of Productivity & Organizing Professionals (NAPO). I've watched far more hours of YouTube on the same subjects than I want to admit. I've also been through my own therapy and coaching. I had a whole transformative experience as a yoga teacher. And I work my ass off to be a more grounded version of myself every year.

☆ SUCCESS STRATEGY ☆

Never apologize for being the real you.

Get ready for a ride! My clients tell me the reason they love me is how real I am. The real me is a rollercoaster of advice, confessions, truisms, and a mouth that would make a sailor blush.

But . . .

I will never tell you to do something I haven't done yet or wouldn't be willing to do.

I'm also a person who is trying to figure herself out day to day just like you. Some days I'm killin' it. Some days I put my underwear on inside out.

You're going to hear a lot about my life partner of twenty-seven years, henceforth referred to as my husband, Shawn. In a side note: He asked to instead be referred to as (in no particular order) Carlos Spicyweiner (*Family Guy* "Something, Something, Something Dark Side"), John Cocktoasten (*Fletch*), Ted Clubber Lang (*Ted 2*), McLovin (*Superbad*), Jake Ryan (*Sixteen Candles* for the ladies), and, ultimately, Batman. I had to shoot him down.

He's my rock, a giant pain in my ass, the smartest, funniest man I've ever known, and, while he will absolutely tell me when he has an opinion about something, he is also fabulously easygoing and pretty much goes along with everything I do in and to our home.

We live with our two calico cats Ruby and Soho (named for Rancid's punk rock song "Ruby Soho"), which means that our tidy little home is perpetually littered with cat toys, cardboard boxes, and hair ties.

You work with the shit you've got.

WHO IS THIS BOOK REALLY FOR?

You. You picked it up, so you must have some stuff to clear out, in your home and in your head.

I don't care if you have one cluttered room or 5,000 square feet of clutter. This book is for you.

It doesn't matter what gender you are; this book is for you. We all have homes. We all deal with clutter. Whether you live solo or share your space, you are responsible for it and for your own mental health.

The days of caring for the home being solely a female role are gone(ish). In my work, I empower everyone to take ownership of the spaces they live in, the children they're raising, and the emotions they're living.

This book is for anyone who has ever felt like their shit was in control of them instead of the other way around.

If you're ready to take control of some shit, this is your book.

WHAT WILL THIS JOURNEY LOOK LIKE?

There is no such thing as decluttering your home once and never having to do anything again.

Have you ever read Marie Kondo's books? You should. She has some great ideas in there. I use a ton of them. However, the sticking point for me in *The Life-Changing Magic of Tidying Up* was when she said, "People who use the KonMari system never revert to clutter again." I didn't then—and I don't now—believe it. It isn't possible (and you'll read later in the book what I think about words like "never" and "always"), so be kind to yourself.

For that to be accurate, it would mean that *none* of her clients ever struggled with the mental and emotional crap of maintaining the decluttered homes and organized spaces they had created with her help.

This is a rollercoaster journey for most of us. Maybe most of Ms. Kondo's clients are simply farther along in their emotional journey than the rest of us. But many people find themselves fascinated by her work, yet frustrated with their inability to follow through on her steps on their own. In all fairness, she does note that many people drop out of her program too.

One plan does not fit all journeys.

You will struggle. That's okay. You will have successes, and you will need adjustments. That's okay. It's okay to acknowledge that after you declutter, there will be areas that get out of control again. The difference will be that if you've done the work in this book, you'll know how to figure out what happened inside yourself, how it impacted the inside of your home, and how to get yourself back on track.

Your home and life will get more and more streamlined with every "relapse" and recovery.

☆ SUCCESS STRATEGY ☆

Take it slow. You aren't going to "fix" yourself or your home by burning yourself out.

It wasn't easy to declutter my own house.

I'm not talking about the physical act of decluttering—that

was easy in comparison to the mental and emotional process I went through.

I had to listen to my own heart and my intuition. "Shoulds," judgments, and preconceived ideas were flying around in my head, and I had to be willing to let them go.

I had to do it for me, not for anyone else. This was my journey. If I had been doing it to please someone else, to prove something to others, to validate my existence, I was not going to be able to sustain my forward motion.

That all applies to you too. I'll keep sharing the things I had to do to stay the course in my own decluttering. Like I said, I'm going to normalize the shit out of you and your experience.

What I can tell you with 100 percent certainty is that all the work I did and all the work you're going to do is totally worth it. You'll find out what I told you at the beginning of all of this: decluttering your home is self-care.

WHAT'S NEXT?

Your next step is to complete your first "Making It Real" exercise. At the end of the book, you'll revisit your answers to this exercise to see if you've achieved what you set out to achieve, if this work has spilled over into other areas of your life, and if you now see yourself and your home in a different light.

So, get ready to dig in. With each chapter of this book, you'll be closer to creating a sustainable plan to finally experience those feelings of relief, pride, and achievement you've been searching for.

Let's get this shit going!

MAKING IT REAL

In the following exercise, answer a few questions to create your "baseline." (At the conclusion of the book, in *What the Actual Shit!? You Did It!*, you'll revisit these questions to see where you've grown and how your life and home have changed.)

On a scale from 1–10 (1 being zilch and 10 being fully enlightened), how self-aware do you feel you are? (Circle your number) **1** **2** **3** **4** **5** **6** **7** **8** **9** **10**	What tells you that's how self-aware you are? ***For example,*** *I feel like I have no idea who I am,* **OR** *I feel like I can usually notice what my feelings are when they're happening.*
How often do you shit-talk yourself? (Circle one) **NEVER** **ONCE IN A WHILE** **ALL THE TIME**	What do you feel the reason is for this level of shit-talking? ***For example,*** *That's just how I was raised,* **OR** *I try to be positive about myself.*

What are three goals you have for yourself? **1.** **2.** **3.**	What are three goals you have for your home? **1.** **2.** **3.**	What are three additional goals you would like to achieve? **1.** **2.** **3.**
What do you think stops you from having a life you love?	What do you think stops you from having a home you love?	What are three awesome things you know to be true about yourself?
What are you looking forward to decluttering the most?	What are you dreading decluttering?	What are you hoping to get out of this book?

PART 1

THE MENTAL SHIT

CHAPTER 1

READY TO CHANGE SOME SHIT?

To begin anything, you have to first know where the heck you are. In this case, where you are in terms of readiness to do what you want to do.

The fact that you're reading this book says to me that you're—at the very least—considering change. That's a great place to start! However, you might find you aren't quite ready to make a plan. Or maybe you can make a plan but find you can't get yourself to take action.

In this chapter, I'm going to get you familiar with the Five Stages of Change. This is the first step in figuring out your shit so that you can take action. That's the whole point, right?

WHAT THE HELL ARE THE FIVE STAGES OF CHANGE?

In 1977, a couple of terribly smart psychologists, James O. Prochaska and Carlo DiClemente, created the transtheoretical model of behavior change. (Don't worry: you don't have to remember any of that; there won't be a test.)

In this model, they outlined five Stages of Change: precontemplation, contemplation, preparation, action, and maintenance. (Again, don't worry; this isn't a stick-up-the-ass psychology book: I'll explain what the stages are, then you can forget the names of them.)

These stages are going to help you understand why you're stuck by identifying where you are in your process of change.

By the end of this chapter, I want you to understand what Stage of Change you're in, regardless of the action you want to take. I want you to be able to see that the reason you could declutter your dishes but can't get yourself to declutter the pantry is that the dishes were what you were ready for. The pantry, however, represents something to you that has you stuck in an earlier stage.

Being armed with that information will help you understand yourself better and judge yourself less harshly for things that seem illogical on the outside.

HOW A BRUTAL BLOW TURNED OUT TO BE THE BEST THING IN THE END

Looking back on my life, it's easy now to see the stages of change in my own experiences.

Like how the universe apparently felt I needed to learn one more big fucking life lesson before I was ready to declutter my own home.

It had nothing to do with physical clutter, and everything

to do with oiling up my rusty mental hinges to move through the Stages of Change.

I had been a skinny kid who could eat anything and never gain a pound. I lived across from the University of Michigan Rec Center for two years and never set foot inside, even though I had been a super-aggressive defenseman in soccer in high school and rollerbladed around campus all the time. I just didn't have the motivation to purposely work out.

In my mid-thirties, when my metabolism started to slow down, I began a workout regimen that started at 10 minutes a day and was up to three hours a day a few years later. No, I don't still do that. Different times in life require different things.

I molded my body into a powerhouse. My vanity was at an all-time high. I loved to be right in front of the mirrors in a workout class so I could see those muscles move. My ego was in heaven.

Then tragedy struck. One day, the owner of the studio, whom I loved, took me aside and let me know she was selling the studio and moving to Florida.

What!? NO. No. Just no. Fuck off. No.

I was stunned. I whipped through a few stages of grief (*see page* 8) right there in the studio: denial that this was happening; begging her to not do it, I skipped over anger and launched into depression.

My whole weekly routine was anchored by my time at this studio with these teachers. I was in a tailspin.

As I slowly moved into acceptance and discovered that someone I knew and trusted was going to take over the studio, I began to realize that what was so disorienting was that I had been forced out of my established Maintenance (stage five), where I had a set routine that literally maintained my physical being, and had been pushed backward into Contemplation (stage two).

I had a problem: something in my life was changing that I had no way to stop. I had to figure out how to adapt.

I moved forward into Preparation (stage three) and began figuring out what all of this meant for me. The previous owner of the studio had been one of my two favorite Pilates teachers, so I needed to find somewhere else to work out, while also maintaining some classes at this place I had called home for so long.

My Action stage (stage four) involved checking out classes at various studios in what we call the Tri-City area of the Chicago suburbs.

This led to all kinds of other changes. I've weaved in and out of the Stages of Change ever since. I learned that change is not a bad thing. In fact, at my new studio I got trained as a yoga teacher, and I met many wonderful friends.

Loss and change are not evil. They're actually the shit that gives us the opportunity to make the greatest steps in our lives, and I will always be grateful for each step of my journey.

THE STAGES OF CHANGE

The Five Stages of Change are kind of like the stages of grief (*see page* 8) in that people wobble in and out of them even after hitting Maintenance (the fifth stage). That wobbling is what our lives are made of. Remember when I told you there would be a cycle where you learned more each time you took a lap around the wheel? This is that cycle.

STAGE 1
PRECONTEMPLATION

STAGE 2
CONTEMPLATION

STAGE 3
PREPARATION

STAGE 4
ACTION

STAGE 5
MAINTENANCE

In my own life story, I have moved through all five stages so often, I can't even count them.

You will do the same thing. This is not bad. You are not flaky: you are trying to figure shit out, just like the rest of us.

☆ SUCCESS STRATEGY ☆

Accept the stage you're in without judgment. This is where you are meant to be at this moment.

THINGS THAT MAKE YOU GO HMMM . . .

While we're talking about stages, let's touch on the five stages of grief too! (Cheerful shit, right?)

Why is it important for a book on decluttering to talk about grief? Because decluttering is about letting go of things. That can sometimes feel like loss. Grief is about loss of any kind, whether the loss of a loved one, an ideal, or an expectation, or even the loss of a butter dish.

DENIAL
is the place where you can't accept that the loss is even happening.

For example: *"Nope, I'm not getting rid of that ugly-ass vase Aunt Norma left me. I don't care what everyone else says. I may not like it, but I can't get rid of it. Are you nuts?"*

BARGAINING
is when you start trying to make a deal to be able to keep the thing you want.

For example: *"Okay, what if I just make sure I clean the kitchen every day? Then I won't have to get rid of anything, right? I mean, I know I keep saying I'm going to clean the kitchen, and don't, but I'll do it this time, I swear."* (*Notice the denial in there too?*)

ANGER
is the emotional place you go to when all of the other feelings are too hard to deal with.

For example: *"I'm so fucking tired of all of this. Why do I have to get rid of my stuff? These are my memories. Stop telling me what to do!"*

DEPRESSION
is just a fancy word for sadness.

For example: *"This is the blanket I brought my son home in. Letting go of it feels like I'm losing the connection to him and losing those memories."*

ACCEPTANCE
is the acknowledgment of reality. When you work with what *is*, instead of what you *thought* it was supposed to be, or *hoped* or *wished* it was going to be, you can finally move forward.

For example: *"Yeah, I get it. I had to let go of those things to have room for the life I want. It's been hard, but I can handle hard. I loved those things, but they were not me or my memories. I'll be okay."*

STAGE 1: PRECONTEMPLATION

When you're in Precontemplation, you might have thoughts like "I have no idea what anyone is talking about. I see no problem here," or "I don't need to or want to change anytime soon," or "I can't."

Like in the stages of grief, denial and lack of insight are hallmarks of this stage.

Ah, denial. What a lovely vacation place. It doesn't create a healthy home, but we all love to visit once in a while.

"I'm just a messy person."

"I've always been like this; there isn't any changing it."

"It isn't my fault. If my wife would just . . ."

So many excuses, so much time. We lie to ourselves out of denial. The lie makes it so you don't have to change. You don't have to do anything. You can pretend it's all okay or it's someone else's fault.

In short, Precontemplation is the place you are when you can't see the forest for the trees. Other people may be able to see that something is wrong with you, but *you* still can't see it. The reason you can't see it is that it's too painful. You stay stuck so you don't have to face all the hard work of seeing yourself for real.

Change is freaking hard.

Thankfully, there are things in your life that will shake up your snow globe and knock you out of denial. Things that create just enough insight to nudge you into the Contemplation stage. That's where the potential for change begins.

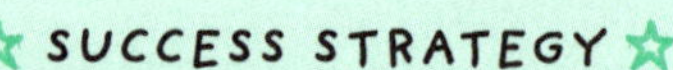

Even if you have to push a new idea away when someone first presents it to you, give yourself the gift of thinking it over later on your own.

STAGE 2: CONTEMPLATION

This is the "There's definitely a problem but I have *no* idea what to do about it, so I'm not going to do anything," or "I'd like to make changes soon, but I feel conflicted about it" stage.

That's where I come in!

Something has shifted. Insight was gained somehow, and you're seeing things differently. Then there it is. Truth.

It's a little vague at this stage. You know something is wrong, but you can't quite put your finger on it. You don't want to poke at it too hard, though, because that might lead to all that icky change stuff.

This is a scarier stage than Precontemplation. In Precontemplation, you were blissfully ignorant. Well, not totally blissful. You weren't happy, but you didn't think that was odd.

Now you're beginning to think it might be odd to not be happy or at least content.

Did you watch a Netflix documentary on minimalism or decluttering? Did you run across a YouTube video that made you think there might actually be something to be done about your home? What did someone say to you recently that flipped a switch? What broke through?

Because now you're in Contemplation, and—while we do move between stages an awful lot—you can't unknow something. Once you know something is wrong, you really can't go back to denial.

SUCCESS STRATEGY

When you make an assumption about yourself or someone else, ask yourself if you know that thing to be true. Do you have evidence that it is true? If not, maybe it isn't.

This is the time to consider the possibility that you might have more control over your life than you gave yourself credit for. This means taking responsibility, which is the really scary part. When you take responsibility, you can't help but notice that you may have had something to do with what's happened.

Like, you probably had something to do with the house getting to the hot-mess place it is now. That doesn't feel good. Now you're realizing that you may have to, literally, clean up your own mess.

Contemplation is when you accept responsibility and see what you have control over. Then you're ready to move into Preparation, because the denial is gone and you want to make things move.

STAGE 3: PREPARATION

At this point, you're getting the itch to do something about the mess you're living with. "There's definitely a problem, I can do something about it, and I'm ready to start planning."

When you get to Preparation, you might be ready to spring into action without a plan. Not a great idea. Without a clear goal and a plan (*see Chapter 6*), you'll get confused and overwhelmed and slide back to Contemplation.

All of this insight and acceptance can be really uncomfortable. Don't worry if you periodically run screaming back to the previous stage. It's an understandable thing to do. Change happens when you're ready to move forward again.

Most of us want change. Not everyone wants the process of change.

I was blown away and totally dismayed the day I heard my seventy-three-year-old father-in-law say he had no interest in learning anything new. As I've thought about it over time, I respect that he knows himself and he knows what he does and does not want. It's the rest of us (me) who think he's supposed to want to change who get all twitchy.

In my journey, I've found that I *do* want to learn. I'm assuming you want to learn, too, since you're reading this. That has to come with the understanding that learning creates change, and change stirs up the unknown, which we do not like. My father-in-law understands this. He is very clear that he likes things to stay exactly as they are.

So, you take control by creating your goal. Something like "I want to feel at peace when I walk through my front door," or "I'd really like to be able to find something in my closet," or "I want to feel comfortable having guests over."

☆ SUCCESS STRATEGY ☆

Imagine a staircase in front of you. At the top of the stairs is your goal. Fill in the rest of the steps.

Take a deep breath. You're only planning at this point. If you feel overwhelmed, remind yourself of that.

Looking at the big picture of Preparation, it's like in the movie *Rocky* when we get an eighties montage of him training for the big fight. He's making a plan based on what he knows of his opponent, technique is being honed, stamina is being built, and he's getting pumped for the main event.

If Rocky went straight from "I want to beat the holy hell out of Drago for killing my best friend" to jumping in the ring, he'd have gotten creamed. Action, without clarity of purpose and a plan, tends to go wildly amok when you least expect it.

If you know your *Rocky* movies, you'll also know that for this particular fight, Rocky trained his way, not the way someone else told him he should. (It involved a lot of chopping of wood, for some reason.) Anyways, my point is, when you're making your plan and preparing for Action, you need to base that plan on who you are, not who you think you're supposed to be.

When—and only when—you are ready (I mean *really* ready, not when you think you *should* be ready, so you say you are), take a deep breath and move to the next stage.

No more contemplating. No more planning. We're moving headlong into Action.

STAGE 4: ACTION

This is the stage everyone thinks they're supposed to be at automatically, but then they become frustrated.

If you skipped or skimmed the first stages and think you should be able to start at Action, you're probably feeling very stuck and very frustrated. Go back and figure out where you really are.

I want you at "I know what's going on; *I have a plan*. Let's do this thing!"

When you've done your work in the other stages and you have a plan based on who you know yourself to be and the circumstances of your environment, go for it. Declutter to your heart's content.

Don't get freaked out when you revisit one of the earlier stages.

If you do run screaming back to an earlier stage, don't worry about it. You're going to do the work in this book, which will make damn sure you come back to Action.

When you're truly ready for Action, you'll feel it. For me it was like a gnat in my ear. If I didn't do the thing I was thinking about doing, it would bug (pun intended) me until I tackled it.

The word *Action* makes it sound like this is a simple stage. It is, and it isn't. Yes, the point is to get moving, to get shit done. But you want to do that in a mindful, planful, and intentional way. When you're in the midst of Action, it can be easy to lose sight of your goals with the heady rush of tasks getting accomplished.

This is the stage when you get to see what you are capable of. Your goals are no longer vague thoughts or sketches on a piece of paper: they're real, tangible, and yours.

As you complete tasks, you'll breathe a sigh of relief and contentment at a job well done.

But don't get too cocky. This all has to be maintained, remember? It's one of the biggest mistakes you can make. It's like going on a diet, reaching your weight goal, and then having no plan as to how to stay there.

You need a plan for Maintenance.

STAGE 5: MAINTENANCE

Don't get too comfortable. There's work to be done after the work. The awesome thing is that you've made Maintenance super-easy because you have a better idea of how you got to the cluttered place to start with, so there's no need to go back there. "I had a plan, I followed through on that plan, and now I get to enjoy the fruits of my labors!" or "It's been over six months since I started decluttering, and it feels pretty automatic now. I have temporary lapses, but I'm mastering how to get back on track and be consistent."

During your Action stage, you will have put some systems in place to make the physical maintenance of your home totally easy.

As you maintain, you'll notice little things here and there to tweak. The more you declutter and organize your space, the easier it will be to see what else can be done because it will be less and less overwhelming.

As before, don't worry if you wander back into previous stages.

Many people tell me they're afraid to start, because they think they'll slide back.

I'll tell you a secret: everyone slides back now and then.

This cannot be about *never* sliding. That implies perfection (*see Chapter 3*), which doesn't exist. It's about what you do when you slide. Do you curl up in a ball of shame (*see Chapter 3*) and self-criticism? Or do you take one of those deep breaths and figure out how to get back on track?

You've shown up to this point that you are totally capable of creating solutions. Don't stop now!

☆ SUCCESS STRATEGY ☆

As my dad said over and over when I was a kid, if it ain't broke, don't fix it.

My only caution is to not overthink it all. Listen to your heart. Sometimes it won't be about making a system better, it'll be about not making it worse by meddling with something that's doing just fine.

To move through these stages and reach your goals, you've got some mental and physical work to do. Now that you know how to tell what stage of readiness you're in, it's time to start dealing with the barriers to your success.

MAKING IT REAL

Before you move forward, take some time to answer these questions to help you understand what stage you're at. You can keep referring back to this as you read this book and take action in decluttering. Your answers will keep changing as you move through your journey!

PRECONTEMPLATION	Is there anything people keep commenting on that you think isn't a big deal?	If you're honest with yourself, do you notice things that you wish were different?	Do you feel stuck, but can't figure out what's gotten in your way?
CONTEMPLATION	Have you begun to suspect that the way you do things might not be producing the results you want?	Do you think you might lie to yourself so you don't have to change?	Are there things others have noted that seemed silly?
PREPARATION	Is there something you really want to change, and you're ready to start investigating how to do it?	Is there a task that you can't get out of your mind, but you know you've got to attend to it?	Do you keep talking about something to other people, telling them what you're planning?
ACTION	Are you actively creating planful and intentional change?	If you're honest with yourself, is what you're doing moving you toward goals, not away from them?	Are you clear enough about what you're doing that you can write a description with clear, concise words? Or is it difficult to explain clearly?
MAINTENANCE	Have you completed a task?	Are you aware there are little adjustments that will need to be attended to with the thing you completed?	Do you have a sense of relief, pride, and accomplishment? Or do you have a nagging feeling that something is missing?

CHAPTER 2

SHITTY THINKING

Now that you understand there are stages to being ready to take on tasks, it's time to talk about the things that hold you back from Action. We'll start with facing your limiting beliefs and fears. Did you just say "Limiting what?" or "I'm not afraid of anything, I just can't get my shit together"? That's okay; keep reading, and you'll understand.

Your beliefs are the foundation of your whole castle. Fear is the most primal emotion we have, and it can control your entire life if you let it. These are the things that make you pretend there isn't a problem to start with or boost you into readiness to start making a plan of attack.

Nothing like digging out the deepest shit first, right?

Limiting beliefs predict ahead of time that you can't do something or you can't be something you want to be. They're the opposite of the stuff that manifests your best life. Fears are the thoughts that lurk in the corners of your mind, making you fight without reason, run away, or freeze in place, never actually accomplishing anything.

Fear is your most primal emotion, telling you how dangerous everything is. Limiting beliefs tell you that you can't face your fears anyway, so why bother trying?

HOW I KEPT MYSELF STUCK

When I began my own decluttering journey, I had to be willing to let myself have a home I wanted.

It seems so simple. Why wouldn't someone allow themselves to have the home they wanted? Isn't it just not doing things right that keeps you from your goals? Nope. Your thoughts and feelings actually run the show.

I believed I was a slob. I believed I didn't know how to keep a home. I believed that what was, would always be. Believing all of that made it hard to let myself have a home I loved. Having that home would contradict everything I believed.

☆ SUCCESS STRATEGY ☆

Awareness is the first step in creating change. Begin paying attention to what you believe to be true about yourself.

If I let myself have the home I wanted, I would have to believe I could be trusted to care for it. I didn't believe that, because I hadn't given myself any evidence yet. I believed that I deserved things I loved, but I had no evidence that I could be trusted with them. I was the person who always sat on her sunglasses and broke them. I was the person who never cleaned behind the toilet (thank the universe for Anna, my cleaning lady/domestic goddess). I was the person who always had a sink full of dishes.

THINGS THAT MAKE YOU GO HMMM . . .

There's a stigma around having a cleaner. When we got one, I felt like we had reached a new level of what my hubs and I call "fuck it." As in, "I have leveled up and I can afford to have someone help me with something I struggle with, so fuck it!"

When I suggest to overwhelmed people that they consider a cleaner, if it is within the budget, I get a number of answers:

"I've thought about doing that so many times, but . . ."

"I feel like that would be saying I can't take care of my own home."

"I'm worried people would judge me."

"Well, maybe I could have someone come in once a year and do a deep clean, but I should be able to take care of my own house."

"I don't feel like I deserve a cleaner, since I should be able to do it myself."

"I'm definitely going to get one...after I declutter the whole house."

"I feel like it might be in poor taste (as in a throwback to British housekeepers like in Downton Abbey*)."*

Do you notice a theme? It's rarely money. It's a fear of judgment, a sense of not deserving. The idea that there's something wrong with you if you don't clean your own house.

Hey, Shawn and I do clean a toilet now and then. We keep the dishes done, the laundry done, the counters clean, the floors cleared, and a handful of other small things. That's enough for us. When Anna comes to clean, it's like a breath of fresh air. It's a weight taken off our shoulders. It isn't like she performs miracles. Well, I thought she had when she turned my old brown tub into a white tub, but that's what professionals do. They do what we don't!

I have never heard anyone other than some catty, jealous "C-you-next-Tuesday" judge someone for having a cleaner. I really hope you don't let the opinions of that sort of person dictate what you deserve.

REASONS ONE MIGHT GET A CLEANER

Kids make it tough to actually clean.

A job takes up too much time to attend to everything.

You don't actually know how to clean a house.

Motivation to get your ass in gear to tidy the house enough so they can get to surfaces.

To show you how nice it is to have a clean home so you want to keep it that way and become motivated to create systems.

And perhaps most importantly:
Because everyone deserves support!

To change those beliefs, I had to let go of my fear. I didn't even know I was afraid of anything! But I was, and the only way to really get over a fear is to do the thing you're afraid of so you can collect the evidence that your fear has no basis.

- ✕ I was afraid I'd fail.
- ✕ I was afraid to disrupt Shawn by changing the rules in our house.
- ✕ I was afraid to find out that if I really could do this, then I'd have to keep it up, and that would prove too much for me.
- ✕ I was afraid to let go of crap I'd given symbolism to and had held on to through countless moves earlier in life.

It's all so clear to me now, but before I really dug deep into my own mental shit, I had no idea how much I was holding myself back.

The truth is that you are capable of having whatever life and home you want. You have to believe you deserve that life and home. Then you have to be willing to do the work and face your fears.

LIMITING BELIEFS

Limiting beliefs are sneaky. You don't always know that they're even there. I had flippantly said "I'm just a slob" for so many years, it didn't seem odd to me at all. As far as my evidence told me, that was the truth.

That's what's sneaky about limiting beliefs—the fact that they feel true to you up until you realize they aren't.

What are your limiting beliefs?

- ✕ That you're a bad housekeeper?
- ✕ You can't organize anything right?
- ✕ You always forget things?
- ✕ That you'll never be able to let go of your grandmother's collection of Hummels?

The beliefs you have about yourself are what tell you whether to work for the life you want or to give up.

WHAT TO DO ABOUT LIMITING BELIEFS

Limiting beliefs don't just go away on their own if you ignore them long enough. Taking control and changing them means you have to acknowledge they exist in the first place.

Willingness is the key to a lot of this. We tend to be a bit willful, digging our little heels in the dirt like donkeys, insisting that we can't change. But change only happens when you're willing to change your thinking. Change "can't" to "can." Change "perfect" to "good enough."

Why do I say "willing"? Shouldn't you be willing because you want it? Nope. Willingness is about being open to accepting what is, instead of wishing for what was supposed to be. Accept the good, the bad, and the ugly without judgment.

Willingness is being ready to do what has to be done, regardless of how uncomfortable it might be.

Let's say your limiting belief is "I can't handle this." Regardless of what "this" is, you're setting the scene ahead of time that you won't be able to handle it. Not that it'll be hard to handle, but that you literally will not be able to handle it.

You've failed before you've tried. But, hey, you predicted your failure, so it won't hurt so badly, right? Nope yet again.

You might think that thinking less of yourself somehow

protects you from the pain of failure. In reality, it doesn't protect you from anything, but it does ensure that you never try. If you never try, then you can't fail. That's messed-up logic. Oh, right, not logic—emotion.

So, you need to bring real logic in. You need to ask questions to ground yourself in logic, to override the reactive defense of emotions.

- How do you know you can't handle this thing?
- Do you have evidence that you can't handle it?
- And what does "handle it" really mean?
- What's another way to say this that's really true?

☆ SUCCESS STRATEGY ☆

Avoid all-or-nothing words like "always" and "never."

How about: "I haven't done this before, so it feels hard and scary. I'm afraid I won't be able to do it and will be judged by others when I fail." Sure, it's wordier, but it's more honest. It's easy to use fewer words and not really think through what you're saying. It's harder to break your limiting belief down and figure out what isn't real and what is.

FEAR

When you declutter, you'll be afraid of a lot of things. You might not think it's fear at first, so let's clarify that feelings like anxiety, worry, and nervousness all fall under the umbrella of fear. When you say "I'm worried that [fill in the blank]," you're really saying you're afraid of something.

If you worry about other people judging you, you're afraid.

If you worry that if you get rid of that scarf you never wear, you'll have a scarf emergency, you're afraid.

In decluttering your home, the fear monster can be a raging beast—or it can be quiet as a mouse. Either way, it will keep you stuck. Some common fears are:

- I might need this someday.
- The person who gave me this might be hurt or mad if I get rid of it.
- I'll regret getting rid of this thing.
- I don't know who I am if I don't have all of this stuff.

You may then get angry because you're so fearful.

You may get angry a lot. Angry with yourself. Angry with the people who have given you things. Angry with your spouse, your kids, the dog . . .

But anger is what we call a secondary emotion. It doesn't happen unless some other emotion happened first, like fear, hurt, sadness, shame, or guilt. That's why I'm not spending a ton of time on it. Anger just covers up the real feelings because it feels more powerful, and less vulnerable, than those other feelings.

Facing fear is really fucking hard.
Don't let anyone ever tell you it isn't.

The fantastic thing is that when you stare fear in the eye and tell it to go to hell, and then take action regardless of the fear, you end up feeling way more powerful and in control than anger ever is.

There's this weird-ass thing that happens when you let go of the crap in your house you've been afraid to do anything about. Instead of feeling bad, you feel empowered. Instead of feeling loss, you feel relief.

☆ SUCCESS STRATEGY ☆

Find one item in your house that brings up a fear and put it in a storage bin in the garage. When you realize you feel better with it gone, get it all the way out of your home ASAP!

WHAT TO DO ABOUT FEAR

Clients usually push back when I ask them what they're afraid of. "I'm not afraid of anything—I'm trying to be logical. What if I regret something I get rid of? Where does that leave me?"

The phrase "what if" is a great warning sign that fear is running the show.

"What if they don't like what I say?" or "What if I need this thing someday?" These questions are a stall tactic and need to be nipped in the bud.

STEP 1: Identify what you are afraid of.

- ✕ I'm afraid they'll judge me if they don't like my opinion.
- ✕ I'm afraid I'll feel stupid for getting rid of this if I need it someday.

STEP 2: Answer the what-ifs.

- ✕ If they actually don't like me because I have a different opinion, maybe I need to rethink who I hang out with.
- ✕ If I really do need this thing again someday, I can either buy another one, borrow one, or improvise a different solution because I'm not an idiot.

STEP 3: Do the thing regardless of the fear.

- ✕ I'm owning my opinion even if I'm shaking inside.
- ✕ Damn, it feels good to get rid of that thing!

You will not get over a fear by simply giving it time.

You will get over a fear by facing it.

That's why, once you've handled your what-ifs, it's time to *do* instead of *think*. "What if I fail? Then I'll learn something and try again. Okay! Here I go, I'm taking the risk!" That brief internal dialogue took you from Contemplation right on through to Action.

Most things will stop being scary after you've experienced them. It's like looking the boogeyman in the face and finding out that he was really just a shadow dancing on your bedroom wall.

☆ SUCCESS STRATEGY ☆

Write down your fears, then take control and shred them, burn them, or rip the crap up out of them.

Go ahead. Stare the boogeyman right in the face and tell him to go to hell. You're the one in charge now, not him and his fear-monsters.

THE TAKEAWAY

This is a lot of mindset-shifting. It's a lot of accepting a different perspective than you've been living with up until now. I'll now point out that the way you've been doing things probably hasn't been working. Otherwise, you wouldn't be reading this book.

You have the capacity to use real logic to get out of your own head. If you just said "No, I don't," that's a limiting belief. It's time to let that shit go.

MAKING IT REAL

When we sit still and accept a life that doesn't fit us, we ensure we can't be happy. To counter that, you need to challenge your thinking and increase your awareness of the thoughts that are running the show.

CHALLENGING LIMITING BELIEFS	What is a limiting belief you have about yourself: **Such as:** *I'm stupid.*	Explain why that limiting belief is true: **For example:** *Because I always make stupid decisions and always screw things up.*
	Now use some logic to explain why that belief isn't true: **For example:** *First of all, "always" is pretty extreme; I don't do anything 100 percent of the time. Second of all, yes, I've made some decisions based on fear or insecurity; but I'm an intelligent person, so I guess I can't be considered "stupid."*	How are you going to use your new perspective? **For example:** *When I make a decision about something, I'm going to check in to see if it's logical or if I'm making the decision out of fear or insecurity. Then I'll think about the possible outcomes and decide whether it's what I want.*
FACING FEAR	Admit to something you're afraid of: **Such as:** *I'll never declutter this entire house.*	Describe the evidence you have that supports your fear: **For example:** *Every time I try to face decluttering, I freeze up and don't get anywhere.*
	Explain why that evidence isn't really evidence: **For example:** *All I know is that I've frozen up and stopped progress when I've tried to declutter before now. I don't actually know that I'll never get this done.*	Describe how you can get real evidence to prove or disprove your fear: **For example:** *I could declutter one small space instead of pushing myself to think about it all at one time. That way, I might be able to see if I really can't handle this or if I've just been taking on too much at one time.*

CHAPTER 3

LET THAT SHIT GO

It's time to talk about some shit you've gotta let go of. Not that extra coffeemaker that never gets used—not yet. First, we're going to talk about letting go of shame and perfectionism, two barriers to happiness that keep you stuck. Sounds like fun, right?

Seriously, though, letting go of stuff is an emotional experience. It can be a relief when you let go, but it can be tough beforehand while you figure out why you don't want to let anything go.

The trick is to recognize that this stuff is not you. It does not represent your value or worth. It is not your memories. It is not your children or your deceased grandmother. Things are only things. Once you get that, you'll be able to let go of the material things faster and faster.

☆ SUCCESS STRATEGY ☆

Ask yourself what evidence you have that this thing you're worried about or feel shame over is true. Use logic to simmer down unruly emotions.

HOW A SUBSCRIPTION BOX ALMOST DID ME IN

We all have our little issues and insecurities we deal with. One of mine has been that I've spent money on ridiculous and unnecessary things. This really got out of control during a yearlong adventure of subscription-box purchasing. I totaled it up once, and I bought over sixty different subscription boxes—and got multiple months of many of them.

Oh, yeah, you thought you were fucked up, huh? Check *that* shit out. BTW, I'm fine, and you will be too.

If you don't know what a subscription box, or sub box, is, it's literally a box filled with a bunch of stuff that goes with a theme, like yoga, skincare, scarves, dried meats; you know, stuff like that. Someone else picks out a bunch of stuff, sends it to you, and now you have to deal with it. Let's just say that I gave a lot away that year.

I mentioned that a possible sub box is one with scarves. I don't even wear scarves! And yet, for a moment in time, scarves became my albatross. Let me explain.

I had decided scarves were going to be my "thing." My signature. So not only did I buy them, I also bought many months of a scarf subscription. You read that right. I was collecting scarves I hadn't even picked out for myself, to fulfill an idea of who I was supposed to be.

They were all so pretty, with organic patterns, soothing colors, and natural materials woven by artisans in Third World countries—all things I value (I'll talk about values in the next chapter).

**When I tried to declutter them,
I ran into a brick wall of shame.**

Over scarves? Hell, yeah. I felt shame over having a subscription to something I thought I was *supposed* to want. I spent money on these things, and damn it, I was supposed to *wear* them, not get rid of them!

Some of that shame was based on the limiting belief that I'm supposed to be better or smarter than that. My own sense of perfectionism created this idea that I wasn't supposed to "fail."

☆ SUCCESS STRATEGY ☆

If you're having a hard time getting rid of something you know in your heart needs to go, put it in a box and set it on a shelf. Set a reminder in your phone for three months out and check in to see if you're ready to let it go.

In the end, I let the scarves go, and in doing so, I let go of the belief that I was "bad" (hence the shame) because I'd wasted money on them. Letting go made me feel lighter and more authentic. I saw that I didn't have to be perfect; I could screw up and still be good enough. Since then, I have not given myself a hard time over money that is already gone. I just get rid of the item and move on.

Side note: I can write about this now and laugh, not cringe. That's how I really know I have totally let go of that shit.

SHAME

My scarf story is a small nugget of the giant house of shame so many people live in. When your home is cluttered, it becomes a glaring symbol of how stuck you feel. You start and stop, and you begin to believe this pattern means something bad about you. You feel embarrassed to have people come over. If they do come over, you desperately shove things into closets and under beds, trying to hide your shame.

Sometimes there's just too much to shove into closets, so you don't even let friends and family come over. If a service person has to come into the house, you find yourself pushing the clutter this way and that to make a path for them to walk through.

The state of your home feels like it becomes an extension of yourself.

You begin to believe your clutter *is* you. That if others see your clutter, they'll judge you just as badly as you judge yourself, which must mean there really *is* something fundamentally wrong with you. Hence, shame.

WHAT TO DO ABOUT SHAME

Every time you say you're embarrassed, you're saying you're ashamed.

When you feel shame, you're telling yourself that you're bad. Not the action or the thing or the event, but *you*. Doing something "wrong" makes you think you are bad.

To process through shame, you're going to have to dig deep.

- Find the originating cause of the shame.
- Figure out what it is about that thing that makes you feel like you're bad.
- Forgive yourself for being human.
- Decide how you're going to proceed.

☆ SUCCESS STRATEGY ☆

When you feel embarrassed, slow down and take a deep breath before saying or doing anything reactive.

In my story about the scarves, my original issue was actually that I felt I had been making poor choices with finances in general. What made me feel like I was a bad person was that the whole scarf thing triggered my feeling that I had made some shitty choices with our money and had created debt.

When I realized that was what was going on, I forgave myself for being human, and I proceeded by giving myself permission to let go of this symbol of my shame.

All that from a scarf? Yes. Do not dismiss your feelings or the real issue just because you think it shouldn't be that big of a deal or that a normal person would suck it up and handle it. The biggest emotional pains can hide in the most unlikely of places.

THINGS THAT MAKE YOU GO HMMM . . .

ANGER IS A SECONDARY EMOTION. "A WHAT, NOW?" YOU ASK.

In a nutshell: Anger doesn't happen first. Another emotion comes before it.

What the hell does that mean? That when you get angry, the anger is not the issue.

The issue might be something like shame. Or other feelings like hurt, guilt, resentment, sadness, and so on. Anger is a nice powerful feeling that you default to when you're feeling vulnerable and icky (technical term!) and you don't like it.

FOR EXAMPLE

Your husband says he's going golfing on a day you had plans with him to go to lunch. You feel hurt, unimportant, and resentful. You could tell him all of this and ask him to follow through on his plans with you. Instead, you blow. "What the fuck!?" you scream. "Why do you always do this? You're such an asshole. I swear, I never should have married you! You don't give a shit about me!"

OUCH.

You felt vulnerable in your hurt, resentment, and fear that you aren't important to him. It felt more powerful to go straight to anger. The problem is, now you're pissed. He's pissed. And no one is rational any longer. When you can recognize the feelings you're actually having, and deal with those head-on, anger is no longer necessary.

THE SOLUTION

1. Describe the event to your husband without emotion: "We had made plans. You changed those plans to golfing without talking with me about it first."
2. Express how you feel or felt using "I" statements (yes, I know "I" statements sound so therapisty and forced, but I swear they work!). For example: "When you did that, I felt like you didn't care about me or about spending time with me. I felt like I'm not important to you, and I felt hurt."
3. Assert what it is that you need. For example: "I need you to talk with me about things like this. I might have been totally cool with you going golfing if we'd talked about it first and made a new plan to spend time together."
4. Reinforce all of this by describing why this is important to you and what the outcomes will be if he chooses (or doesn't choose) to work with you. For example: "It's important to me to feel like we're partners. If you can do this for me, I know that I'll feel more loved and less hurt, which will lead to less reactivity from me."

Bonus: Then you can ask the question: "Is that something you can do for me?" I love this question, because it creates either a verbal contract when he says "yes" or a new line of conversation if he says "no," leading to more clarity and communication.

BTW—This method is adapted from the Interpersonal Effectiveness strategy called DEAR MAN from Dialectical Behavior Therapy (DBT).

PERFECTIONISM

I've seen perfectionism go a couple of different ways. Either a person is so focused on being perfect that they live in a museum-like home, or they're so frozen by perfectionism that their home is a disaster.

Neither of these extremes is healthy.

But that's the thing about perfectionism—it's all about an extreme that doesn't exist.

Perfect isn't a real thing. To be perfect, something has to be without flaws. Not even something that has been made by a machine is perfect. All things have flaws.

**If you try to aim at perfection,
you've failed before you ever begin.**

The first time I use the "P" word with clients, they almost always reject the crap out of it. "I'm not a perfectionist. Have you seen what a mess my home is?" BTW, those who have the museum-like homes aren't exactly seeking my services as a decluttering coach, but I do hope they have a good therapist.

Perfectionism doesn't mean your home or life is actually perfect. It means you keep trying to make something that will always have flaws—no matter what—be flawless. Even a flawless diamond isn't flawless!

☆ SUCCESS STRATEGY ☆

If you aren't sure whether you're doing the perfectionist thing or not, start paying attention to how often you think things like "I can't do that until I can do it all." Words like *always, never, all, completely, right,* and even *perfectly* can be signs that you're doing some all-or-nothing thinking.

To have a home that you love and that you can relax in, you're going to have to be willing to risk not being perfect.

I had to take the risk to let go of those scarves and my beliefs about myself. At the time, it really did feel like a risk. In the end, letting go of the extremes and the scarves, I felt better. Totally worth it.

WHAT TO DO ABOUT PERFECTIONISM

Like I said, you're going to have to be willing to take a risk. This is the point at which most people throw something to distract me and start running. Why would I be so cruel as to suggest they *not* be perfect!?

Isn't "perfect" how you know you're good enough? Nope.

I want to give a nod to Tal Ben-Shahar, the author of *The Pursuit of Perfect*. He talks about perfectionism vs. *optimalism*. Love this idea!

Optimalism is doing things at the optimal level you have available to you right now. That level may change day to day; but, in this moment, you're going to operate at your optimal level. Therefore, you are no longer aiming at perfection, which doesn't take your current energy or vulnerabilities into account.

Ben-Shahar discusses the 80/20 rule too. If you've ever followed me on social media, you'll have heard me talk about the 80/20 rule, because it's awesome.

To fully appreciate the awesomeness of the 80/20 rule, you have to accept the idea of "good enough."

If they haven't run screaming from me yet, this is the next point at which people abandon ship. It's just too much to bear—to even consider the idea of going from perfect to good enough.

It's unfortunate, but good enough has gotten a bad rap. I can't tell you how often I've been told that good enough isn't good enough, a concept that makes my head hurt.

Good enough is, by definition, good enough!

Look, I get that our culture has developed this idea that good enough is like being a C student. Average. Sure, you passed the class, but is it anything to be proud of?

Yes! You freaking passed the class! Do a dance, throw a party!

The 20 percent that is beyond good enough is a bonus.

Aim at 80 percent. If you get more than that, cool. But if you don't, don't punish yourself. You're amazing. You're a super-cool human being. And, like the rest of us, you're average. You're good enough as you are. I'm good enough as I am. That person sitting in Starbucks working on their novel, too, is good enough. (Shout-out to all my fellow authors, burning it at your local coffee shops!)

Your home is good enough too.

As long as you keep thinking your home isn't good enough, you're going to feel gross and you aren't going to want to do anything about it, as in declutter, clean, or organize.

> ☆ **SUCCESS STRATEGY** ☆
>
> **Ask yourself what's realistic. Not what's ideal. But what's real.**

When you embrace decluttering at 80 percent, you give yourself permission to fuck it up. Honestly, I don't know *how* you're going to fuck it up, but you have permission now.

When you embrace optimalism, you'll give yourself permission to be human: to have tons of energy one day and zilch the next and to get done whatever is in line with that energy level.

The next thing you know, you'll be decluttering because you're no longer frozen by the fear that you aren't going to do it right.

THE TAKEAWAY

Shame will make you want to curl up into a ball and never do anything.

Perfectionism will freeze you in place because you will never meet your own expectations.

But none of this is going to happen, right? You're going to declutter your life and home, because you know that the state of your life and home is not a reflection of your value. You're going to operate as an optimalist. You're going to aim at 80 percent, knowing that, if you get more than 80 percent, it's a bonus.

In the end, shame, perfectionism, limiting beliefs, fear, and a million other barriers will rear their ugly little heads. That doesn't mean you're doing the wrong thing, that you should stop, or that you should give up.

If it's important to you, you keep going.

MAKING IT REAL

In this exercise, you're going to sit with some uncomfortable stuff. It's an exercise you can do over and over to help you when you get stuck in shame and fear. The discomfort is worth it when you get to the other side.

SHAME	**1.** What is something about your home that you feel embarrassed about?	**2.** What is it about that thing that really feels icky (as in shame-filled)?
	3. What is the logic you need to hear to tell you that this thing doesn't define you?	**4.** How do you want to handle it now?
PERFECTIONISM	**1.** What is something you keep not doing because you're afraid you're going to mess it up?	**2.** What would it look like if you did that thing at 80 percent?
	3. What is the limiting belief you have that is stopping you from aiming at 80 percent?	**4.** What would it feel like to finally get that thing done, even at 80 percent?

CHAPTER 4

WHAT SHIT DO YOU VALUE?

When you're trying to figure out what's important to you, you have to examine your values.

Do you value honesty over power? Do you value loyalty over success? Your values shape the way you interact with the world. If you value honesty higher than most other things, you will hate it when others lie, and you'll hate yourself when you do.

Your core values will dictate what material things you value too. If you value family highly, you may find being surrounded by photos of your family—or reminders of them—makes you happy. If you value wealth, you may have a home that oozes the high-end items that signify luxury. If you value honesty, you will hopefully have a home that is authentically a reflection of you, whoever you are.

In this chapter we're going to talk about values, what they are, what gets in the way of them, and how to live by them.

ONE OF MY VALUES IS TO DO WHAT I TELL YOU TO DO

When I went through yoga-teacher training, I faced a lot of emotional stuff and got closer to understanding myself. I got closer to seeing what I valued instead of what I thought I was supposed to value. It's no coincidence that I decluttered my home around the same time that I started teacher training.

I was already living a life that was more and more geared toward my values, and my home was beginning to reflect that.

Yes, I value hard work, but I value quality time with myself and my loved ones more. So I began balancing things in my life better by giving myself a morning every week to be by myself. I worked on better boundaries with work so I could be present when I was with those loved ones instead of being half somewhere else.

I had burned myself out by not paying attention to what I truly valued. When I started paying attention, I began to get myself back from wherever I had gone.

Today I reevaluate and recommit to my values weekly, if not daily. It isn't perfect, and I certainly lose track of myself now and then, but now I know how to bring myself back.

☆ SUCCESS STRATEGY ☆

Be gentle with yourself as you try to figure out what your values are (not what you think they should be). It's an ongoing process, and while your core values may not change, the level of priority they each have may.

My home reflects this. It's free of excess crap that I don't value. I'm slowly redesigning my home to fit who Shawn and I are by taking one room at a time and mindfully changing things.

I thought for the longest time that I didn't know how to decorate a home. The problem wasn't that I couldn't picture three dimensions (as I told myself); the problem was that I wasn't clear as to who I was and what I valued.

My home is filled with pictures of my travels with my husband and posters from our favorite bands and concerts we've attended. My bedroom is a sanctuary of peace, and my home office looks like a yogi works there, with my yoga mat hung by the door with a singing bowl, and sage to burn. Oh, yeah, and there are cat toys *everywhere.*

I didn't think I could ever love this house. For the longest time, it didn't seem to have a personality. But all I really had to do was understand myself so I could love me. The personality of my home is mine and Shawn's. The clutter had just been covering that up.

Now we live surrounded by what we value.

LIVING BY YOUR VALUES

First you have to know what you value. This requires a shitload of honesty from you, so I'm hoping honesty is somewhere in your top five values.

The honesty required is the willingness to acknowledge what *you* value, not what someone else you admire values or what you think you're supposed to aspire to be like. Maybe you grew up in a house where a value that was modeled was being thin no matter what, but you were not born with a body that adheres to this value easily and you would have to do some harmful things to yourself to measure up to that value.

You might come to realize that, regardless of the urgings of your upbringing and your family's continued behaviors, health is of more value to you than body shape. This would probably require a lot of courage to stand up for. But being honest with yourself about valuing health over body shape would be what gives you the freedom to live a happier, more satisfied life.

Examples of core values are:

Family	Wealth	Knowledge	Achievement
Education	Creativity	Honesty	Community
Power	Loyalty	Authenticity	Kindness
Recognition	Wisdom	Trust	Security
Money	Independence	Respect	Spirituality

THINGS THAT MAKE YOU GO HMMM . . .

Knowing what your core values are means you get to live an authentic life, yay! Okay, maybe you've heard "authentic life" as some sort of hippie-dippy catchphrase, and it seems a little too "woo" to really put thought into. But I'm telling you, this authentic-life stuff is the bomb. It's where happiness lies. And that's what we're all about in this book, right? Finding your happy place. An authentic life is one in which you are you, unapologetically.

Check off all the things that apply to how you are living your life.

☐ I stand up for myself, even if it might not be the popular thing to do.	☐ I'm not afraid to fail or make mistakes.	☐ I listen to my gut, even when old messages in my head tell me to doubt myself.	☐ I'm honest with myself, even when I don't like it.	☐ I can make decisions without asking other people what they want.
☐ I've started noticing things just coming together, like it was meant to be.	☐ I deal with shit head-on, instead of avoiding it until it blows up in my face.	☐ I accept my limitations and don't give myself a hard time because of them.	☐ I learn from everything I do, especially the things that blow up in my face.	☐ I don't bother worrying about shit I have zero control over.
☐ I let people know what I'm feeling.	☐ I can't remember the last time I got into gossiping around the water cooler.	☐ I don't see the point in complaining anymore. I decide whether things are worth dealing with or ignoring.	☐ I've let go of the need to be pissed off at anyone who hurt me in the past.	☐ I no longer bow to social pressures if it doesn't feel right to me.
☐ I follow my passions and give myself a sense of purpose by doing so.	☐ I'm willing to listen to what other people say, even when I kinda think they're nuts.	☐ I don't look to anyone but myself to make me happy. If someone else does, that's a bonus.	☐ I actually believe in my ability to do shit.	☐ I really do like my own company.

Give yourself a pat on the back for the one(s) you checked. Think about the ones left over. Which stand out as something you would really like to focus on to take the next steps toward your authentic life?

THE ENEMY OF VALUES

There are things in your life and in your home that drain your energy. These are things that are in conflict with your values. Energy-drainers could be things like unfinished projects. They could also be things like relationships you don't enjoy.

Anything that creates negativity for you is an energy-drainer.

The fact that you're reading this book tells me you value having an uncluttered home. Therefore, clutter is going to drain you. Yup, it's that simple. The stuff that is stopping you from living the life you want to live is draining your energy.

Some possible energy-drainers to get you thinking about what might be draining in your life are:

- Your job
- Your home
- Lost items
- Self-criticism
- Traffic
- Unfinished projects
- Laundry
- A critical parent
- Time
- Debt

When your energy is drained, you can't live the life you want. You have no motivation because you have no energy. You may find this seeping into all areas of your life, like not eating well, not getting enough sleep, not moving your body, or accepting less than you deserve.

Then you have less energy to give to the things you do value, like the home you are living your life in.

☆ SUCCESS STRATEGY ☆

Take a wander around your house and notice the things that tug at your eye or whose presence you can still feel after you've walked past them. These are drainers to be attended to.

We often ignore energy-drainers and just keep looking for more things to increase our energy. The problem with that is that all of the energy drinks and Om symbols in the world cannot overcome things that are draining you.

You have to remove the things draining you in order to be able to create space for the beautiful things that you're doing to have a chance to help you.

Then and only then will you truly be living by your values and creating the life and home you've always deserved.

VALUES AND DECOR

Houses come in all shapes and sizes. There are so many design and decor styles out there, I can't keep up. I told my mother recently that I had decided that the style I was aiming at for a remodel on my kitchen was "farmhouse industrial."

Now, I had made this term up, but it was still fun to have her response be "WTF is that!?" (It was a text, and yes, I get my trucker-style language from my sweet, petite mother.)

Whatever style of home you live in, I'm guessing your friends' homes have different styles than yours. Perhaps one person values bright colors, while another values subdued neutrals. One person may value open-concept minimalism, while another may value a small bungalow filled with all of the things that make them smile. One may value a bohemian style and what it represents about them, while another values mid-century modern with its clean lines and simplicity.

Which of these people are wrong? Which are right? So long as they are being authentic about what they love, they are all right. There is no wrong answer when you follow your heart and what you value.

☆ SUCCESS STRATEGY ☆

Use Pinterest. If you're looking to decorate, use the tools social media has provided. Get boards together. Find colors you like. Find styles that ring true. It will all come together.

You may recall that I had mentioned my previous belief that I had no ability to decorate a three-dimensional space. I now feel totally at ease decorating my home. I have no anxiety about it: I totally trust my decisions. Why? Because I'm living authentically and not questioning who I am and what I want.

It's freaking awesome! Man, I want you to feel that too. So let's get this values-based decluttering going and get one more step closer.

VALUES AND LIFE AND GROWTH: OH, MY!

Like I've said, decluttering is an emotional experience. Have you gotten that feeling too? You will run up against what you value over and over again. You will question if what you value is right or wrong. You will be fearful that others will judge what you value. You will face the fact that what you value has changed over time, as your life has changed.

One friend of mine got stuck in her decluttering when she came across all the super-cool makeup she had painstakingly purchased when she was younger and a baby aesthetician. Gorgeous colors, glitter, rare items, and lots of money spent.

It wasn't the stuff that was the problem; it was what it represented.

She was running up against the values of a younger version of herself, who was single and searching for her identity. The woman she was today, a mother, wife, business owner, yogi, hair stylist, aesthetician, and overall super-cool human, had shifted her values.

☆ SUCCESS STRATEGY ☆

When you feel anxiety creeping up in you as you consider letting go of something, ask yourself what it symbolizes to you. Decide how important that symbol is.

She had to face the fear of what it meant to declutter the symbols of those values, which belonged to a different version of herself, while also identifying which values still applied since she was technically still the same person. There was even some grief involved, as it felt like she was losing the version of herself that felt more free and independent. Yeah, super fucking emotional.

She gave herself time and slowly chipped away at it. Finally, she came down to a small handful of her faves. Regardless of her admission that she was unlikely to wear glitter any more than maybe once a year, we let her have it. It gave her joy to see those pretty flecks.

She got to that place because she accepted the life she has now, which, by the way, she loves.

She just needed to see that she was still herself, and she needed to evaluate her values and priorities as they applied to her life today.

As you declutter and get stuck now and then, ask yourself, "What does this item say about my values overall and what I value specifically?" Then decide if that applies to the current authentic version of yourself. That will help you decide the fate of the item.

THE TAKEAWAY

Your home is your sanctuary. It isn't just a box you live in. You do not have to have a large home or a lot of money to have your home reflect your values.

You also don't have to have a small home and little money to prove your values to anyone.

If you look at my home, you can see my values of travel, experiences, my relationship, fun, coziness, quiet, work, yoga, cats, and a ton more. Before I decluttered, you may have gotten some of that if you looked hard enough, but it wasn't until I had cleared space for my values (oh, yeah, and those of my husband!) that they were truly able to shine through.

When you live in a home that is counter to your values, you'll feel drained, which will suck up your motivation and lead to a dissatisfying life.

Create a life and home that are all about who you are, what you love, what fulfills you, and what simply brings you joy. Do that, and all the tough stuff will be easier to face because you won't be dealing with a bunch of extra crap first, like that handful of shitty habits I'm sure you've been holding on to for dear life.

MAKING IT REAL

Let's figure out the values that guide you. Complete this worksheet to help give you an overview of yourself and help you figure out what you're doing all of this for.

Number these 20 values in order of importance to you:

_____	Family	_____	Wealth	_____	Knowledge	_____	Achievement
_____	Education	_____	Creativity	_____	Honesty	_____	Community
_____	Power	_____	Loyalty	_____	Authenticity	_____	Kindness
_____	Recognition	_____	Wisdom	_____	Trust	_____	Security
_____	Money	_____	Independence	_____	Respect	_____	Spirituality

Take your top five values and explain why they're important to you:

For example: *Kindness, because I've found that kindness toward others makes me feel good, and I have less need to be angry when I prioritize kindness.*

1.

2.

3.

4.

5.

List five things you're grateful for and why:

For example: *Peanut butter, because it's delicious and makes a fabulous evening snack on a spoon.*

1.

2.

3.

4.

5.

Write out ten things that are draining your energy:

1.	**2.**	**3.**	**4.**	**5.**
6.	**7.**	**8.**	**9.**	**10.**

Choose three of those drainers that you want to take action on, and why:

For example: *The pile of papers at the top of the stairs that never dies, because it makes me feel like a slob and a failure every time I pass it. (Real example from my pre-decluttered life.)*

1.

2.

3.

CHAPTER 5

DITCH YOUR SHITTY HABITS

You're a smart cookie. If you're honest with yourself, you know what most of your shitty habits are. I'm guessing you know exactly when you're doing something that doesn't help you and might even be hurting you.

That's what shitty habits are: the things you do that sabotage your life.

They're the things that move you away from your goals. They're actions or thoughts you do over and over, knowing they're slowly killing you.

For example, dismissing compliments is a shitty habit I see all the time. Hell, I've worked my ass off to accept compliments myself, but now and then I still have insecure moments that make words come out of my mouth from a long-ago habit, dismissing the gift I was just given.

☆ SUCCESS STRATEGY ☆

When someone compliments you, say "Thank you" and move on with your life. They don't need to know every reason you think they're wrong.

Another example might be getting up late every day. This causes you to rush, which makes you forget something you were supposed to do. Then you don't eat breakfast, can't figure out what to wear, and get pissed off at other drivers on your way to being late for work.

Hell, simply buying stuff just because it's on sale, not because you want it, need it, or will use it, is a shitty habit.

In other words, shitty habits are disruptive habits. They get in the way of you having a life and home you love.

Up to this point in the book, we have addressed:

- Limiting beliefs
- Fear
- Shame
- Perfectionism
- Values

Now we're going to get into how all those things create barriers to success and a shit ton of craptastic habits that drag you down and keep you stuck. Ready? Come on, this is going to be fun!

HOW A SHITTY HABIT GOT OUT OF CONTROL

Okay. At the beginning of this book, I promised you a really horrifying story, so here it is. This is an example of how things can get out of control when you don't pay attention to your own shitty habits.

In my early twenties, I lived in a little apartment in Chicago with my long-haired black cat Oliver. I didn't have a dishwasher, so the habit I had developed living in my little efficiency apartment in college of leaving dishes in the sink for days, even weeks, was still going strong.

One hot Chicago summer, I left to visit my dad for a few days, leaving that sink full of dishes to welcome me home.

What I didn't realize was that I had left a can with a small amount of wet cat food in it, sitting on the counter next to the chaos in the sink.

Not only had I let that blend in with the other crap around it and not tossed it in the garbage bin, I hadn't even emptied my garbage before leaving. The shitty habits kept piling up!

☆ SUCCESS STRATEGY ☆

Have a checklist for all the things that need attending to before leaving the house for the day or a vacation, so you don't have to keep it all in your head.

If you have a delicate stomach, stop reading now and go on to the next section. This is bad.

When I got home from my trip, the can was still sitting on the counter. But now it was moving. Yes, moving. In the few days of my absence, it had become a breeding ground for maggots.

My skin crawls telling you this.

Yeah, that might have been a clue something was not quite right in the way I was keeping my home.

I wasn't ready to make changes yet, so it would be years before I realized I could actually do something about my habits.

About a year later, Shawn and I moved into a little apartment together. I got better about not leaving dishes in the living room, because the habit bothered him and I didn't want to make his home uncomfortable. Cat-food cans weren't being left out anymore, but he didn't have much better habits than I did when it came to dishes, so the sink continued to be full all the time.

Then we bought our first house and admitted the depths our shitty habits had taken us to, and splurged on hiring Anna, our cleaning lady/domestic goddess.

We needed help, and bless her little heart, Anna was very kind about dealing with our crap. She would even do the dishes for us! If an area of the house got too cluttered, she would kindly ask that we do something about it so she could actually do her job. This was how we held back the tide for years.

When I went through my decluttering journey, one of the first habits I changed was the dishes thing. I now run the dishwasher at night, empty it right after my morning yoga practice, feed my two very verbal calico cats, and then wipe down the sink and counters.

My motivation is how great it feels when it's all tidied and cleaned. Unhelpful habit gone; helpful habit established.

SHITTY HABITS DON'T DEFINE YOU

Having crappy and unhelpful habits does not make you lazy, stupid, or bad. Everyone has at least one or two, if not fifty, habits they need to wrangle. Everyone.

Remember what I said about shame rearing up because you think you're bad when you *do* something deemed bad? Crappy habits leave you extra vulnerable to labeling yourself as bad.

Habits do not define you. They impact the fuck out of your life, but they do not define you.

For example: if you walk into the house and drop your coat on the floor instead of putting it in the coat closet, it's likely a habit you want (or someone you live with wants) changed. It would be easy to say you're just lazy, but what we call laziness always has a reason behind it.

More often than not, a habit like this comes from some form of attention deficit. You walk into the house, get distracted, the coat drops, and in your distraction, you forget about it.

This is not a character flaw.

A new habit can be put in place to stop this from happening in the future, like having a coat hook immediately inside the front door, instead of trying to get all the way to a coat closet. But it doesn't make you a better person to change the habit, just like it doesn't make you a worse person for not changing the habit.

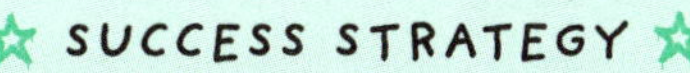

Identify the least complex solution to a problem. The more steps there are, the less likely you'll be to follow through.

If, like my former self, you have a sink full of dishes all the time, you are not a bad person. I've embraced this, which is why I can tell you my stories shame-free. You just need to find a system that works for you, and probably deal with some limiting beliefs (*see Chapter 2*).

My limiting belief with the dishes, and cleaning, decluttering, tidying, etc., was that I was a "slob." Always had been, always would be, so there was no reason to work on it, right?

Clearly, I was wrong. Plus, I was the same fabulous person when I followed a slovenly routine that I am today with all of my shiny new helpful habits.

Unhelpful habits weigh you down and give you ammunition against yourself. We're going to change that.

SOME SHITTY HABITS TO LOOK OUT FOR

My clients run into a lot of the same themes in their barriers to success. Since you're as beautifully human as any of them, I figured I'd share four of the most common barriers I've come across.

OLD LABELS THAT WON'T LET GO

You already know that my old label was "slob." Other people have said their labels are things like "failure," "bad mom," "failed adult," "stupid," "terrible husband," "incapable," "messy person," "disorganized," etc.

When something is a label, you use it to define yourself. You need to get real clear with yourself as to what your current label(s) is/are.

If you don't give yourself permission to release the old labels and create some new ones, you'll keep repeating all of the crappy habits you've built because you'll assume you're incapable of change.

One client finally quit smoking by changing her label to "a person who doesn't smoke." Any time she had an urge, she reminded herself that it didn't make sense, because she was a person who didn't smoke!

LIES, LIES, AND MORE LIES

We lie to ourselves all the time. "I don't have time" is a super overused one. Stop using your busy life as an excuse.

I empathize with the busyness of your life. This world has evolved to go way faster than our brains are truly capable of functioning.

You have the ability to prioritize everything else; therefore, you can learn to prioritize yourself.

"I can't" is another big fat lie. What bullshit! Drag your sorry ass out of self-pity, and actually freaking try. I mean *really try*. Not that half-assed crap that supports all of your limiting beliefs and gives you an excuse to give up.

You can do way more than you give yourself credit for.

ABSOLUTES LIKE "NEVER" AND "ALWAYS"

Whine, whine, whine. "I'll always have a disorganized house," "I'll never have a home as nice as [insert twenty of your closest friends]." Says who?

Always and *never* rarely actually apply. Think about it. What can you really say always happens? What can you say never happens? You can take a minute to come up with an argument to my hypothesis. I'll wait...All I ask is that when you come up with something, you ask the question: "Is that really true?"

Absolutes have no place in your life.

When you feel like ass, I promise you will not *always* feel that way.

When you worry that you'll never be able to learn a new skill, the only reason that would be true is if you didn't ever try.

NEEDING TO CHANGE OTHER PEOPLE

Get ready to kick and scream at this one. I get so much shit over this from clients who don't believe it's possible to sit by and let other people do things they deem wrong without trying to "fix" it.

When you start a decluttering journey, the other people in your home may not be ready to jump on the change train with you.

This journey isn't theirs, it's yours.

Declutter, tidy, and organize because it's important to you. Teach your children new ways of doing things, of course. But don't waste energy getting pissed at your partner because going through their closet isn't important to them. If they become inspired by your actions, cool; if not, figure out how to live together with respect, not with the expectation that anyone is supposed to change for the other person.

☆ SUCCESS STRATEGY ☆

Pay attention to the things you think and start questioning them. Just because it's an automatic thought doesn't make it correct.

THINGS THAT MAKE YOU GO HMMM . . .

So, what the hell are "good" habits? They're things that move you toward the life you want to be living. If that's still a little too vague, let's take a look at a list of habits you could consider working into your life and go from there.

Take a look at this list of habits that organized, productive people tend to have.

Mark anything you already do with a **1**.

Mark anything you want to do with a **2**.

Mark anything you hadn't considered before with a **3**.

Mark anything you think is a little ridiculous with a **4**.

____ Start your mornings early	____ Plan your week ahead of time	____ Plan each day ahead of time	____ Stick to your routines	____ Resist multitasking
____ Use the 80/20 rule	____ Set your workspace up before starting	____ Set your clothes out the night before	____ Willing to say no	____ Create and honor deadlines
____ Accept and really consider feedback	____ Prioritize tasks	____ Eat mindfully	____ Have an intentionally positive outlook	____ Don't bother with perfectionism
____ Delegate tasks	____ Honor your energy levels	____ Only hang with positive people	____ Avoid procrastination	____ Use daily affirmations
____ Journal daily	____ Be realistic about time	____ Take real breaks	____ Get consistent sleep	____ Get consistent physical movement

Now note all of your **1**'s. Nicely done.

Make a list of your **2**'s and put a star by the top three you'd like to focus on.

Make a list of your **3**'s and put a star by one that you might be willing to give a go.

One by one look at your **4**'s. Ask yourself what makes it necessary for you to be judgmental of these ideas. Now ask yourself if you'd be willing to try one of them. Put a star by it.

You aren't going to try all of these new things today. You're going to try one, get it rolling, then add in another. Congratulations: you just took another step toward a happier life!

HOW TO CHANGE A SHITTY HABIT

I know, I was a little rough on you in that last section. I don't agree with being hurtful or cruel to other people or to yourself to create motivation. I do believe in honesty. My clients get the benefit of building a relationship with me before they get subjected to my form of tough love. Consider yourself privileged. People pay a lot of money to get that kind of brutal honesty out of me.

Now that I came in hot and ripped you a new one, let's get solution-focused so you don't have to deal with that crap again.

What's the secret to changing a habit? Practice, practice, practice. Reassess. Practice, practice, practice. Reassess. Repeat as many times as needed.

Changing a habit is the same thing as learning a new skill. You don't expect yourself to be able to play the piano just because someone once explained some music theory to you, right? You take lessons and practice. Then you give yourself credit for your progress and don't go comparing yourself to someone who has had more time, instruction, and practice than you.

Without consistent practice, new habits will not stick.

I work with clients who try over and over to create change. For many, they peter out after about two weeks. They do this over and over and wonder why no change ever sticks.

To have the motivation to maintain consistency, you also have to have done all the previous work in this book (and keep doing it) so you can figure out what is important to you, who you are, and what you're ready to work toward.

☆ SUCCESS STRATEGY ☆

Every time you do something—anything—ask yourself if this is moving you toward or away from your goals.

Here's how I break down the process of habit-establishment:

STEP 1: Implement a change.

STEP 2: Keep doing it, even when it gets hard, irritating, boring, or frustrating around the two-week mark.

STEP 3: Pay attention to whether this new habit is—or isn't—working for you and adjust as necessary to make sure it's a habit based on your personality, not some old "should."

STEP 4: Keep going past the twenty-one-day mark (which a lot of people think is how long it takes to build a habit).

STEP 5: Recommit as often as necessary.

STEP 6: Ask for help when you need it.

STEP 7: Notice as you reach the two-month mark that it isn't as hard as you thought it was before.

STEP 8: Pat yourself on the back and keep going.

At two weeks, the shine has come off the apple and the work begins. At twenty-one days, you're getting into a groove, but you can't take your eyes off the road. At two to three months, a habit will be established enough that you'll notice it feels weird to do something different.

But six months is the brass ring, where a light goes on in your brain, and you realize the thing you've been working so hard to make a habit has somehow turned into one and you didn't really notice.

For example: I swore I'd never make my bed.

I didn't have anything against made beds. When I'm on vacation, I love coming back to a made bed in the hotel room. "Turn-down fairies," as I call those angels who turn down your bed and put a chocolate on your pillow, are my favorite.

But I had a block against doing it myself. It would take so much time to do every morning. Ugh. And isn't it better to air the bed out by not making it? Oh, yeah, I said that.

Then I ran an experiment and started making my bed (which takes approximately three whole minutes when timed) for an initial time frame of 30 days.

It turned out I enjoyed the outcome so much that I kept on going.

That's how I built a habit, stuck with it, and now get to feeling twitchy if the bed *isn't* made.

That's the sort of shit I'm talking about. If I can do it, I swear you can too.

"But, Kate, it's hard. What do I do when I don't feel like doing it?" Oh, dear, you aren't going to like the answer to this: You do it regardless.

"But, Kate, if it was that easy, we'd all set new habits!" I didn't say it was easy. I said do it. Kinda like Nike.

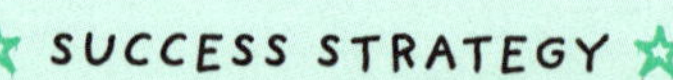

Set goals for new habits that you actually give a shit about.

When I don't want to get out of bed in the morning, I say, "I'm choosing to get up." It works—mostly. 80/20, people. I'm human. But I do stand by the "do it anyway" thing.

Just because something is hard doesn't mean it's impossible. You have to find your "why."

Why get up? Why declutter? Why put the ketchup back? Why work out? Why drink another glass of water? Why go to work in the morning? Find your answer.

My answer to "why bother getting up in the morning" is that I want to feel better. It works—mostly.

WHAT CHANGING HABITS LOOKS LIKE IN YOUR HOME

There's a fun domino effect when you declutter a space and feel proud of it. Feeling proud gives you warm fuzzies that you'll want more of, so you'll want to keep it up. Honestly, it's the same receptors that drugs trigger in your brain. You want the dopamine that is released naturally when you accomplish something because it's a sweet little non-harmful high you get to ride.

To keep getting your fix, you have to put systems of organization in place that keep it that way. The next thing you know, it's bye-bye, shitty habits.

But seriously, that's the way it works. Declutter, feel good, organize, feel even better, maintain.

Pain and fear are great motivators in the short term. Threaten your kid with no dessert, and he'll put his video game down (hopefully). Become fearful of your mother seeing your house a mess and you'll do a massive clean before she comes over. But without pleasure, which is the long-term motivator, your kid will keep going back to his video game and your house will keep turning into a disaster.

Pride, relief, peace, calm...these are positive motivators that keep a new beneficial habit in place.

When I had a decluttered and organized kitchen that made me feel proud and satisfied, I wanted to keep it that way. That's why the dishes kept getting done. Then, with the dishes done, I wanted more, so I followed advice from The FlyLady (flylady.net/d/getting-started) and began "shining" my sink (wiping it down). Then I remembered my mother always said part of doing the dishes is cleaning the counters, so I started wiping them down as well.

☆ SUCCESS STRATEGY ☆

As you build habits, connect them to preexisting habits. Eventually it will seem natural to do B after A, and C after B.

And, voilà! Three new habits were born! I was so amazed by this new world that I couldn't stop talking about it. After every meal, I'd put the food away, load the dishwasher, get it going, and then wipe things down. Because of the lack of excess clutter, and the implementation of systems, it was so easy and fast that I remarked on it over and over, earning a confused look of "yeah, duh" from my (very appreciative) hubby.

That habit in the evening bled into the morning, and systems were slowly put in place. Over time, I've finessed it, and today I have a morning routine that I'm completely dedicated to.

I swear you can do this too.

You are soon going to join the "Gee, That Was Easier Than I Thought It Would Be" Club that so many of us have already joined. We can't wait to have you!

In the second part of this book, I'm going to give you pointers and skills to declutter and organize. With those in your arsenal, and all this mental work in process, you'll slowly begin changing habits you thought you couldn't control.

You're going to be proud of yourself in a way you never knew was possible!

THE TAKEAWAY

Okay, so let's be real and admit that a lot of us have or have had some super-shitty habits. No one is immune. Therefore, you don't suck because of your shitty habit.

It was super-gross that I'd let the dishes get so out of control, but it didn't lower my personal value. Maybe people would have judged me if they'd known, but it didn't make me a bad person: I was still working at the optimal level I had available at the time.

Today I have more to offer. I thought I was a slob, for goodness' sake! And I was so wrong.

Habits are changeable. People are changeable.
You can control that change.

It's going to take work, time, and commitment, but you are no different than any of the rest of us. You can have the life and home you want. Create your goals based on the shitty habits you're currently rocking, and let's get some shit changed!

MAKING IT REAL

To change a habit, you have to be aware of the habits that are holding you back and be honest about how much impact they have. In Chapter 6, we're going to talk about how to set achievable goals; so, for now, you're only going to focus on getting hardcore in your honesty with yourself about the habits that are keeping you from the life you want.

What is a habit you have that keeps you from your health goals? ***Example:*** *Eating in bed before going to sleep.*	How long have you been doing this? ***Example:*** *Almost every night for the past three years.*	What have you already tried in order to change this habit? ***Example:*** *Not taking food with me when I go to bed.*	If you're honest with yourself, what gets in the way of successfully changing this habit? ***Example:*** *Not wanting to give up the comfort I get from bringing food to bed with me.*
What is a morning habit you have that keeps you from starting your day off on the right foot?	How long have you been doing this?	What have you already tried in order to change this habit?	If you're honest with yourself, what gets in the way of successfully changing this habit?
What is a habit you have when you come home at the end of the day that is getting in the way of your evening goals?	How long have you been doing this?	What have you already tried in order to change this habit?	If you're honest with yourself, what gets in the way of successfully changing this habit?

What is a habit you have that helps you procrastinate and not get the crap done that you want to avoid?	How long have you been doing this?	What have you already tried in order to change this habit?	If you're honest with yourself, what gets in the way of successfully changing this habit?
What is a habit that keeps clutter accumulating in your house?	How long have you been doing this?	What have you already tried in order to change this habit?	If you're honest with yourself, what gets in the way of successfully changing this habit?
What is a habit that stops you from having the time to get shit done?	How long have you been doing this?	What have you already tried in order to change this habit?	If you're honest with yourself, what gets in the way of successfully changing this habit?
What is a habit you have that gets in the way of prioritizing yourself?	How long have you been doing this?	What have you already tried in order to change this habit?	If you're honest with yourself, what gets in the way of successfully changing this habit?

CHAPTER 6

GOALS TO GET SHIT DONE

I know, you've done a lot of mental heavy lifting up until this point, and you're itching to get to the hands-on decluttering. But you have one more thing to consider before I set you loose upon your home: how to set goals you can actually reach.

I bet you've set yourself up for failure before by setting goals that were unrealistic or too unclear to reach. You know, all of those things you look back on and ask yourself why you never followed through or finished. That's what I'm talking about.

Knowing how to set a goal can make or break you.

That's in life as well as in decluttering. Most of us never had anyone explain the mechanics of goal-setting to us. So you try and you fail, over and over, while looking at other people and wondering "Why are they able to do all of this and I can't?"

You've faced your inner self and understand your readiness

for change. Now you'll create the goals and the plans to reach those goals to bring that change about. Soon, you'll be the one people look at and are amazed at how you get things done!

HOW I SET GOALS AND ACCOMPLISHED MY DECLUTTERING

When I started my own decluttering journey, I had to set a goal too. Initially it looked like this: "I want to get this shit out of my house."

It was a good place to start, but not terribly focused.

So I changed it to "Over the next three months, I will declutter this house."

I was getting more specific, which meant I was on the right track. What my goal ended up being was:

1. I will touch and make determinations about at least 90 percent of the items in my home.
2. As I declutter each space, I will create new systems of organization to maintain its new tidy state.

Each space and each day came with more specific goals and boundaries that helped me achieve my overall goals in two and a half months for a three-bedroom, one-and-a-half bath, 1,400-square-foot, two-story house with no basement.

I didn't do the garage at that time because I live in the Midwest and I started this in February. It was way too cold to be mucking around in my garage. I saved that for a day in the early summer. I have to redo the garage every year because it gets full of dirt and dried leaves, and it manages to become disheveled faster than any other area of my home. (Hmm, maybe my systems need updating...)

> ☆ SUCCESS STRATEGY ☆
>
> **Plan around the seasons. Heat, cold, daylight levels, pollen levels, smog, rain, moon phase, school being in session or not...any of these things can impact what makes sense to do, as well as your mood to do them.**

The reason I could come up with such a clear plan and follow through on it so thoroughly was because I had already done all of that mental heavy lifting the previous chapters have walked you through.

I had spent years working on my health and my relationship with my body, my mental health through therapy, and my spiritual health through yoga. I was primed to do the physical work in my house, even if I didn't realize that was going to be the next step until I was stepping.

Trust me, if this reformed slob can declutter the crap out of her house, so can you.

WHAT IS A GOAL?

Webster's dictionary defines a goal as "The end toward which effort is directed, something that you are trying to do or achieve."

Doesn't sound too tough, right?

Webster's goes on to provide synonyms for the word "goal": "Aim, ambition, aspiration, dream, end, idea, intent, intention, mark, meaning, objective, plan, point, purpose, target."

I want you to keep these words and this definition in mind as you move forward in creating your own goals.

I want you to be clear with yourself as to what your aim is. To be honest with yourself as to what you want to put effort toward, not what you think you *should* put effort toward.

Think about the purpose of the task you have set before yourself. Is it to make yourself happy and your life easier? Or is it to avoid the judgments of others? The first one will keep you motivated; the second will make it peter out after that two-week time frame discussed in Chapter 5.

Visualize your target or objective.

- What will your home look like when you have achieved your goal?
- What will you feel like when you have achieved your goal?

Visualizing helps you create greater clarity as to what the goal is. If you visualize a home that is always spotless and you have five kids, that isn't realistic. Instead, visualize a home that fits you and those five kids and is easier to care for because it isn't filled with extra crap.

What a goal is not: an unattainable concept built on perfection and other people's ideas of what your life should look like. That's a great way to sabotage yourself.

Constantly creating ideas of what you think goals are supposed to look like without taking yourself, your life, your personality, your needs, and your strengths and weaknesses into account is a setup for failure.

That isn't why you're reading this book.

You're here to figure out how to cast aside all the shit you've been slogging through all these years that has held you back from the life you want. So, let's set some goals.

GOAL-SETTING STEP ONE

BE CLEAR ABOUT YOUR GOAL

When a client comes to me and says, "I want to declutter my house," I say, "Great! What does that mean to you?" They usually pause for a minute and then describe something like a home that they don't feel trapped in or a home without so much crap all over the place. This is a great place to start.

Most people are nervous that they're going to do it wrong or say the wrong thing. Here's a secret: There is no wrong goal, so long as it's *your* goal.

STARTING WITH CLARITY

Let's take a moment right now to think about your goals.

STEP 1: Come up with the prettiest sentence you can to describe your goal.

STEP 2: Write it down. Put a note in your phone. Scribble it in the margins of this book. You're going to come back to this first idea later.

Now I want you to get more detailed.

STEP 3: Describe what that goal means as if you were talking to an alien who has no clue what you're talking about. If your goal is "I want to declutter my house," you might clarify it like this:

I will get rid of anything that:

1. I don't like.
2. Doesn't get used anymore.
3. Is an unnecessary duplicate.
4. Is broken.

With this clear description or set of rules in mind, you'll be able to refer back to it over and over again to know whether or not you are moving toward your goal.

STEP 4: You can get even more detailed, if you like, by writing down what defines something that doesn't get used anymore. Is it clothing that hasn't been worn in a year? Or kitchen gadgets that have dust on them?

In my house, there are a handful of mugs and plastic cups that don't get used, but Shawn will not part with them. They don't take up a ton of space, so I have allowed them to be exempt from the "doesn't get used" rule—for now.

STEP 5: What are the exceptions to your rules? Be careful with this one. Be minimal and clear about any exceptions, otherwise you may find yourself with far too many loopholes and you'll be back to where you started.

An exception I have made is that my husband doesn't want to get rid of it and I'm not interested in controlling what he does or doesn't want.

GET SPECIFIC

In my goal, I noted that I wanted to touch 90 percent of my belongings. Once I had done that, I knew I had met that goal. Well, I also felt I was "done" (you're never really done) because there wasn't anything else glaring in the house to deal with.

Note that I did not set a goal of perfect decluttering. That would have been an unattainable goal and a setup for failure. You don't do that anymore either, right?

I set small daily goals for myself like "Declutter the cabinets in the blue room."

We have a catchall room that has been painted bright blue since we moved into this house in 2005. It's easier to call it the blue room than the "workout/guitar stuff/hubby's crap/office supplies/printer/precious books" room.

In that room, I have four side-by-side cabinets that held a mixture of all those things I just listed and then some. On the day that the goal was to attack them, I:

1. Emptied them out.
2. Tossed everything I could.
3. Piled the questionable things that belonged to my husband that I wasn't going to make decisions about.
4. Reorganized with bins and categories.

This created a new goal, though: Get hubby to go through the pile of goodness-knows-what on the floor. It took about six days, during which I never pressured him, only asked once or twice (nicely) that he get to it, explaining that until he did, I could not meet my goal, which was important to me. Once he did it, most of it got tossed and only a couple of things needed to be slid into the new organization.

☆ SUCCESS STRATEGY ☆

Don't be a dick. Seriously, no one wants to do stuff that you order them to do, guilt them into, chastise them into, or generally make them feel crappy about.

You might have all kinds of different goals. Just make them clear:

- Drop off donations today before picking the kids up from school.
- Separate the winter clothes from the summer clothes.
    - Declutter the winter clothes on Tuesday.
    - Declutter the summer clothes on Friday.
- Pull the stove and refrigerator out to clean under them before two o'clock today.

As long as you have a clear definition of what it means to be done with the goal, then you have clarity about what the goal is in the first place.

You would know you were done with dropping off the donations when they were out of your car. You would know you were done separating the clothes when you had gathered every item of clothing in the house and divided them into two piles. You would know you had dealt with the fridge and stove when those tasks were accomplished.

Be clear.

THINGS THAT MAKE YOU GO HMMM . . .

Whether I'm talking about decluttering or about life, one of my favorite questions to ask when making a decision is:

"IS THIS MOVING ME TOWARD OR AWAY FROM MY GOAL?"

Simple, right?

If your goal is to be more kind, yelling at a store clerk would be moving you away from that goal. Being patient and speaking with kindness and empathy to that same clerk would be moving you toward your goal.

If your goal is to declutter your underwear drawer today, screwing around with other nonessential crap in the house would be moving you away from your goal. Opening the drawer and pulling out the contents would be moving you toward your goal.

Make sense? It's a fabulously simple concept that isn't always easy to adhere to.

Things that move you toward your goal feel great.

Things that move you away from your goal leave you feeling twitchy and weird.

All of the mental shit that you're going through in this first part of the book is what will make it a hell of a lot easier to ask that question, answer it honestly, and move forward.

GOAL-SETTING STEP TWO

KNOW HOW YOU'RE GOING TO GET THERE

If the goal you set for yourself isn't something you can actually do, then you won't be successful. You'll know that fact in your subconscious, which will make your motivation swirl down the toilet.

Saying I wanted to finish my decluttering in three months was achievable; my home is small, and my life is structured so that I could tackle small goals on workdays and larger ones on weekends.

KNOW YOUR LIMITS

Saying you are going to declutter a six-bedroom, four-and-a-half-bath home, while working from home and caring for three kids, in three months is not likely to be achievable—unless you have some fabulous help and systems of organization already in place for your daily routines that allow thirty minutes to two hours a day for decluttering.

First you'll create your realistic big goal, then you'll create your realistic sub-goals. While the big goal may be to declutter the first floor by the end of the month, sub-goals for that might be day-to-day.

To do this:

STEP 1: Sit down with your calendar and see what you have going on in the next month.

STEP 2: Decide which days are going to be decluttering and organizing days.

STEP 3: Determine how much time is realistic to use on each of those days.

STEP 4: Create a master list of everything that needs doing on the first floor.

STEP 5: Slot tasks into the time slots in achievable chunks.

Know how much you can lift. Know how much energy you have. Know what you have the capacity for. Then you know what you can achieve and what is asking too much.

Set yourself up for success by being honest about what you can and cannot achieve.

Then be flexible. The original plan may not happen as expected. You might get the flu and not be able to do any work for a few days. Your kids may have school or extra-curricular activities no one bothered to tell you about ahead of time. Basically, life happens.

Do not let life get you so frustrated that you stop productivity. If you hit a road bump, slow down, inch over it, then resume your original plan once you're beyond it.

Do what makes sense for your life.

I told you in my story that I did not make my garage a part of my goal because it wasn't something I was going to do, due to the cold weather. I made that a completely separate goal at another time that I did not connect to the initial decluttering and organizing goal.

Saturdays, when the kids are stuck inside playing due to inclement weather, are not the time to declutter the play room.

Saying you'll get an hour of work done every weekday when you work 40-plus hours, have a commute, and are freaking exhausted at the end of your day is not taking your life into account.

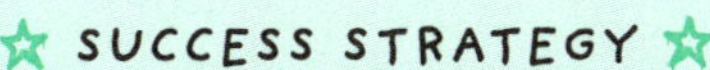

Try stuff out. Run experiments. Who the hell am I to tell you your plan isn't realistic? Just be willing to adjust if you discover it isn't.

KNOW HOW MUCH TIME IT WILL TAKE

Have a realistic time frame to reach your goal. Asking yourself to get ten hours of work done in two hours will leave you exhausted and frustrated.

Three months was totally realistic for my goal because:

- I have a small home.
- I do not have children.
- It was a time of year when I tend to have few social engagements.
- At the time, I was only running one business that required little attention outside of work hours.

If I were to set that same goal today, I would probably have to spread it out over six months or cut down the expectations for that three-month period. My life is different now. Not worse, possibly better, definitely fuller.

Now that you know what your goal is and how you're going to get there, you can guesstimate the time, as long as you're honest with yourself.

STEP 1: Determine how much time the task will take. Minutes? Hours? Days? Weeks?

STEP 2: Decide how much time you have available to commit on a daily or weekly basis.

STEP 3: Divide the time it will take by how much time you have.

For example: If you want to declutter your closet and you believe it will take about eight hours and you have thirty minutes available every day, understand this project will take sixteen days. If you have four hours on Saturday and four hours on Sunday to commit to it, then it will take two days.

Two days sounds way better, right? But if you set that as your goal and you don't actually have those four-hour blocks or you don't have the energy for four hours of decluttering in one day, it won't work.

Be honest with yourself.

☆ SUCCESS STRATEGY ☆

Pretend you're a contractor estimating the time for a project. We all know it takes at least twice as long as any contractor ever estimates, so pad your timeline too.

Maybe you need to divide that closet goal up into more pieces to give you smaller wins in the time you have. Tops one day, bottoms another, shoes the next, accessories after that, and let your spouse deal with their own stuff.

I have a client, Katie, who is a teacher. She has little to nothing to give energetically ten months out of the year. But when summer comes, we hit the ground running!

At the beginning of each summer, we sit down and create a plan for her weeks. We decide on a theme for each day, like self-care day, or socializing day, or decluttering day(s).

☆ SUCCESS STRATEGY ☆

Write out your plan. Do not be so foolish as to believe you'll remember everything. No one ever does. Plus, writing things out makes them more concrete for your brain to process.

Katie rocks out one big declutter and organizing project each summer. One year it was her garage. I want to say she spent about twelve-plus hours getting through everything. Once it was all gone, she had the floors finished and the walls painted and created an art studio for her husband on one side of the garage and a shoe storage/yoga studio for herself on the other side. She was in heaven. She got there with phenomenal planning and execution.

**There is no universal right answer—
there is only the answer that works for you.**

THE TAKEAWAY

To achieve the goals you have, you will need to be planful, mindful, intentional, and honest. You need to:

- Know what your goal is.
- Be clear and specific with it.
- Know your limits.
- Know how much time it will take.

Assess and reassess as you go. This is *your* goal, not someone else's. Make it personal to you. Use everything you've learned in the previous chapters to help support the goals you want to achieve.

Are you ready to put all of this into action? You're about to work your way through your home and then some.

You're going to have lots of shit to sort through mentally and emotionally, as well as all that clutter, of course. You're going to set some realistic goals and start making this dream a reality.

Let's start this bitch!

MAKING IT REAL

Okay! Ready to make a realistic, honest goal that you'll actually achieve? Let's do this.

STEP 1: IDENTIFY THE GOAL.	What goal do you want to work on? ***For example:*** *Revamp my morning routine to allow for a daily walk.*
STEP 2: CLARIFY THE PLAN.	Write out your plan in painstaking detail. For example:

1.	2.	3.	4.	5.
Get up	*Get dressed*	*Make the bed*	*Wash my face*	*Brush my teeth*
6. Sift kitty litter	*7. Feed the cats*	*8. Dishwasher*	*9. Wipe sink*	*10. Go for a walk*

It's okay if you don't need ten steps, or if you need more.

1.	2.	3.	4.	5.
6.	7.	8.	9.	10.

STEP 3: IDENTIFY BARRIERS.	What are the stumbling blocks in your plan? ***For example:*** *Not getting up early enough, scrolling on phone.*
STEP 4: FIGURE OUT THE CAUSES.	What is the real, honest reason those barriers continue to exist? ***For example:*** *My cats get in bed with me and I want their love; so I'm worried if I get up, I'll disrupt their bond with me. Also, dicking around on my phone is sooo much easier than getting up.*
STEP 5: CREATE SOLUTIONS.	What are your solutions? ***For example:*** *Get up regardless of the cats and get over it. They'll be fine. Put my shoes on as soon as I get dressed to give my brain the message that it's "go" time.*

PART 2

THE PHYSICAL SHIT

CHAPTER 7

LET'S DECLUTTER SOME SHIT!

This is so exciting! You're ready to start the physical decluttering! (I know that mental/emotional stuff was rough, right?)

This is the rock star section of this book. It's where my amazing decluttering expert colleagues focus the most. We all want to be here. This was the goal of all that previous work.

Here's the bad news first (I always want the bad news first, so I can be cheered up by the good news): You aren't done with the mental shit. Sorry. Oh, wait: no, I'm not sorry. You're gonna do great!

WHAT TO EXPECT IN PART 2

In the second half of this book, you're going to work your way through your:

- Kitchen
- Bathrooms

- Common areas
- Bedrooms
- Clothing
- Storage areas
- Sentimental stuff

In each of those chapters, you're going to apply all of the shit you just learned. You didn't think I'd let you off the hook and suddenly let this become your average decluttering book, did you? Hells no. You're creating lasting change, remember?

In each chapter, you're going to focus on:

- Stages of change
- Limiting beliefs and fears
- Shame and perfectionism
- Values
- Habits
- Goals

Then at the end of each chapter, you get to process each of these concepts and set some goals.

> ☆ SUCCESS STRATEGY ☆
>
> **Take a pause and a deep breath after each chapter. Don't get overwhelmed by information and ideas.**

WHAT TO EXPECT IN THIS CHAPTER

This chapter is your intro to the physical shit. Think of it as the foundation to return to as you deal with the actual decluttering process.

I'm going to walk you through physical steps to take, as well as things to think about as you declutter.

Decluttering is a step-by-step process. The process needs to be as clear as the home you're creating for yourself. When you have systems, processes, and rules, you have things to fall back on when you become overwhelmed and lost.

☆ SUCCESS STRATEGY ☆

When decluttering feels too overwhelming, fall back on the one-in-two-out rule. Bring one thing into the house, and two must leave. It ensures steady progress. When you're maintaining, you'll shift to one-in-one-out to keep the status quo.

MY PROCESS

Everything I'm sharing with you in this half of the book is from the knowledge I've gathered, the trainings I've taken, and, most importantly, my experiences.

When I began decluttering my own home, I did it with the help of YouTube, podcasts, and books. Through these, I learned the things I didn't know I needed to know, like how to create systems, how to properly clean things, and how to organize a decluttering project so it wasn't overwhelming.

I Frankensteined the process by pulling from all of my resources and creating a system that worked for me. It was hit-or-miss at times, and I had to redo some stuff, but listening to my gut was my best guide.

My hope is to save you some of that. However, you have to make this your own in the end, so a little Frankensteining may be necessary.

I began by creating what I called my Master List (creative name, I know). This was a list of anything and everything I thought of that I wanted to do in the house.

- Blue-room cabinets
- Jeans drawer
- Refrigerator
- Pantry
- Under the upstairs sink
- Paper pile at the top of the stairs
- Steam-clean the window tracks

Things like that. They varied in size and involvement, meaning one thing might be a quick task at the end of a work day and another may have been a Sunday afternoon deal. I kept this list in my phone. I found it helped to have the ability to scroll through the list when figuring out what I wanted to tackle.

When I had some free time, usually a little each day and more on the weekends, I would think about my time and energy availability, and then I would scroll with my gut.

I let my internal radar identify what felt right.

Not what I thought I should do, or what I was dying to get to but didn't have the time or energy for. I'd stop on one, check in with my gut, see what it had to say.

To do this, I paid attention to my mental and physical responses to the task I was considering. If I had a big reaction, like my throat closed up, it was easy. The more subtle responses took more patience and awareness. I had to accept when something didn't feel right inside me, even if I couldn't tell you what that thing was.

Any time I ignored that internal response, I regretted it. I'd end up not having enough time, not feeling motivated, or getting distracted.

You might think this would be a great way to procrastinate the tough jobs, but it wasn't. I wanted to do all of this for myself, so each thing on the list was something I wanted to see get done.

Steam-cleaning the window tracks was a pain in my ass, but I did it because I was excited to see them so clean. However, I ran out of steam (See what I did there? Clever, right?) and only got to the first floor on day one.

"Just do the upstairs while you have the steamer out," my ever-helpful and supportive hubby said. "No," I replied. It didn't require a discussion. I would, and did, get to the upstairs on another day when I had the energy and motivation.

I had to learn to trust myself. I had to figure out that I was doing these things because they were important to me, not because I felt like I should do them to prove something or to be something.

BEFORE-AND-AFTER PHOTOS

Before you start a decluttering project, it's a great idea to take some photographs. Over the course of your tidying, you'll forget what it looked like before. Comparing the "before" pictures to the "after" will give you a great sense of pride and accomplishment.

I wish I had done this when I overhauled my home. My kitchen counter in particular, which we all know was a trigger for me, is now a mystery in my memory. I know there was stuff up there, but what? It's kind of like childbirth: you know it happened; you know it was one hell of an experience; but you can't quite remember the extent of the pain, and the details are a little fuzzy.

Whereas in childbirth not remembering it all is how many women manage to have more than one child, in decluttering remembering is how you can see the growth and fully appreciate the changes you've created.

Point being: Learn from my mistakes. Take the damn photos.

THE FIRST LAYER

Before you can get to the primary clutter, you have to remove those first layers of crap. Don't bother dusting or wiping down anything yet: it's wasted effort. Instead, put your energy into these three first steps every time you start a new project or area:

1. Clear the trash.
2. Clear the broken crap.
3. Clear the unused stuff.

TRASH

This is the stuff that you call garbage, and yet it sits around your house instead of in the waste bin.

I see two primary issues with trash:

1. Little bits of garbage like candy wrappers, receipts, or junk mail just sit around not getting thrown out, even though everyone agrees it's trash.
2. The idea that you should be able to come up with a use for stuff that is actually trash or the perfect solution for getting rid of it (like where the recycling goes if you don't have a weekly pickup).

First of all, time how long it takes to pick up a piece of trash and toss it in the garbage bin and realize how silly it is to not start a new habit of throwing things out when you see them.

Second, remember what I said in Chapter 3? Let that shit go. No more perfectionism to get in your way. You may have to do a few things in a less-than-perfect manner to simply get started.

BROKEN CRAP

I'm all for fixing things and using them instead of buying something new every time something stops working or you blow the seam of your favorite T-shirt. However, there is a limit.

If you actually do fix the things that break, cool! If you let them sit around taunting you, not so cool.

That plaster eagle lamp that fell over and broke into twenty crumbly pieces? It'll never be the same. Let her fly to the great beyond. (My friend Bill had that thing sitting on a table for months before he admitted the truth. RIP eagle lamp. You served him well.)

It's that "honesty with yourself" thing again. If you haven't fixed that one thing in over a year, chances are you aren't going to do it. Tossing the things that break is not a failure; it's realistic.

Besides, broken things block the flow of energy in your home, keeping it stale and gross. Get rid of a few of those "I'll get to it later" projects and see how your energy feels.

UNUSED STUFF

Yes, as you get deeper into your decluttering, you're going to find a ton of shit you never use. And there is a layer of unused things that just sit around being ignored that you aren't attached to and can get rid of fairly easily.

That crystal punch bowl that's been gathering dust since 2005? Gone. Oh, was that just me? I did buy a gorgeous crystal punch bowl with a matching ladle when we bought our house in 2005. I was so sure I was going to be making punch all the time for guests. Apparently 2005 was when the party punch bubble burst. I used it once, at our housewarming party, and then it sat on top of the kitchen cabinets, collecting grease and dust (bad combination). It was one of the first things I decluttered and, man, did it feel good!

Take a look around you and notice the things that have become white noise but you'd love to ditch.

That Keurig that's been sitting unused for three years? Gone. That used gaming console you got to play that one game online with your buddies? (That was Shawn's.) Gone.

These are things that your eye has caught on many times in the past and you've wanted to get rid of, but you just haven't taken the steps to do it. Now is the time. These quick wins will really whet your appetite for more.

PULL IT ALL OUT

Once you've gotten rid of that first layer or so of crap, whatever you are working on needs to be fully emptied to properly declutter it.

Touching your stuff is a huge part of decluttering.

Think about all the crap you haven't touched in years. If you come at decluttering with the mentality of continuing to not touch everything, you'll do a half-assed job of it. One thing we want is to do this whole-assed.

I inadvertently tested this theory with the first closet I decluttered in my house.

I thought I was smarter than every decluttering expert, so I didn't completely empty the closet under our stairs—where all the random household crap lives.

Paper towels, extra toilet paper, extension cords, pet food, vacuum, board games, Jacuzzi supplies—you get the idea. Random.

I pulled out basket after basket, decluttered them, and rearranged them. I went through the board games and determined which ones we might actually use. Eventually, each thing in the closet did leave and then go back in, but I didn't empty it completely. To quote Julia Roberts in *Pretty Woman*: "Big mistake. Huge!"

At the end of my decluttering of the house, I had to go back into that closet and do it properly. I had learned a lot over my journey and could see, every time I opened the door, that it was not truly decluttered.

☆ SUCCESS STRATEGY ☆

Do not be afraid to go in and redo something. Just don't be too perfectionistic about it.

"You just did that one!" Shawn cried out in dismay. (He had begun to live in fear of the disruption of decluttering.)

"Yes, but I didn't do it right," I told him.

Rolling his eyes, he walked away while I dug in. And it was totally worth it.

If you decide you're only decluttering one shelf, that's fine, but you still need to take everything off that shelf before you get going.

THINGS THAT MAKE YOU GO HMMM . . .

MANAGE YOUR EXPECTATIONS OF YOURSELF

You only have so much time and energy at any given moment. You've got to be realistic about how much energy you have and how much time things will take.

Setting realistic expectations will set you up for success. Expecting yourself to do more than you have time and energy for sets you up to peter out partway through, leaving yet another unfinished task in your house.

Unfinished tasks are how you got here! Knock it off.

If you have fifteen minutes, figure out what you can do in fifteen minutes. If you just worked a double, you need to eat and then go to bed—decluttering isn't going to happen. Plus, if you're short on energy, you won't be thinking straight, and you'll make more of those half-assed decisions.

Whether it's day-to-day or week-to-week, be intentional about what you plan to get done.

Write down what you want to get done.

Look at what you have to get done in life today/this week.

Figure out where your pockets of time and energy are.

Fill in tasks that match those pockets.

There will be some days when you get nothing done beyond the daily expectations of life. There will be other days when you have three hours of free time and you can dig in like a tick and get shit done.

QUESTION YOURSELF

To determine whether or not you're keeping or tossing something requires logic. Emotion will try to butt its head in and screw with you, but logic helps solid decisions. Balanced decisions come from equal amounts of emotion and logic.

Think of it like a Venn diagram where you have a logic circle on one side, emotion on the other. That slice in the middle where the two circles overlap is where you want to live. Think of it like Goldilocks: not so logical that you're icy, not so emotional that you're chaotic, but just right.

> ☆ SUCCESS STRATEGY ☆
>
> **Have a trusted friend who has no opinions help by handing you things to make decisions about. That takes away one decision (what to pick up next), which reduces decision fatigue.**

To get more logical in your decision-making, you can ask yourself a series of questions until you come up with an answer.

QUESTION 1: Do I love this?

This is where Marie Kondo's "Does this spark joy?" comes from. You're working on creating a home you love, so it has to be filled with things you love. Pick the thing up and listen to your gut. It will tell you if you love it or not. Trust that feeling.

QUESTION 2: Do I use this?

I get it, not many people have feelings of love for something like a garlic press. So, consider the level of use it receives. If you press garlic weekly, you use that thing and you're keeping it. If you haven't pressed any garlic in years, the press needs to go. If you have a garlic-pressing emergency later, you can get a new one, borrow one, or just mince it.

QUESTION 3: Do I have more than one of these?

If there is a reason that loops back to the previous question and explains why you have multiples of something, great. But if you have six liquid-measuring cups, it's unlikely that you're going to cook something that requires that many separate cups. Again, see the previous question. Decide which ones you do use. Get rid of the rest.

THINGS THAT MAKE YOU GO HMMM . . .

No touch! Do not declutter other people's stuff. Full stop.

Over the three months of decluttering my home, I touched about 90 percent of the stuff in our house. That final 10 percent? I was aware enough to not try to declutter my husband's stuff. I knew that would be a bad, bad idea, and I respected him too much to prioritize decluttering over his sense of safety in his own home.

The three main categories of people in your life that you may be tempted to declutter without permission are:

YOUR SPOUSE

Thinking you know better than your partner about their stuff and its value is one thing. Taking action without their permission to get rid of it is a boundary crossing. I can't guarantee your partner will ever declutter their stuff. If they don't, all you can do is corral their belongings.

YOUR KIDS

It can be argued that under a certain age, parents do need to take control of the decluttering of clothes and toys. Be aware of your kids' need to know what to expect and to have some sense of control over their belongings.

When I was twelve, my mother sold my Transformers at a garage sale without asking my permission. I still haven't gotten over it. I'm just sayin'.

Even small children can be involved in decluttering. They will often even enjoy the process and be better at it than you.

That being said, I do understand there are times when decluttering toys they no longer play with when they aren't home can be beneficial, as children sometimes become reattached to toys when they see them again. Use your best judgment.

FRIENDS AND FAMILY

Just don't. Please. Leave them alone. You're excited and that's cool. I totally get it.

That doesn't mean you now have permission to tell everyone else they should be ready to declutter. Model through your own decluttering experience and let them figure it out when they're ready.

I have a friend who keeps begging me to take on his wife's closet. I've been there, I've seen it, she's seen my face. I say nothing. Until she asks for support, I'm not doin' nuthin'!

You can try this tactic with your spouse and kids:

Bring the items into their view.

Hold the items up one by one and ask what they want to do with them, the options being toss, donate, or keep.

When they become distracted and don't respond, patiently get their attention and begin again.

Repeat as necessary.

Stop when they need to stop.

WHAT ARE YOU KEEPING?

Once everything is pulled out of the space you're decluttering, it's time to start sorting.

It's tempting to think of decluttering as getting rid of stuff. That's fine sometimes, but that can get upsetting and overwhelming. Sometimes thinking about what you're keeping feels more positive.

Did you know that when Michelangelo carved sculptures, he saw it as removing the marble that was covering up the sculpture? He made decisions as to what was clutter and what he was keeping.

This is your work of art. Decide what you want to still be there when the clutter is gone.

The day that a client shows me a space that is half empty because she is being picky about what gets to go back, I shed a tear of pride. That means she gets it. She's really thinking about what is meant to be in the space.

"I'm beginning to question whether I even want any of the stuff I haven't put back yet," one client told me. "I thought I had decluttered, but the idea of putting some of that stuff back on the shelves doesn't feel right. I think I have to reevaluate my 'keep' pile."

Ugh, so fabulous!

☆ SUCCESS STRATEGY ☆

Put things back in their home in stages. Put the most important stuff back first. Step back and take a look at it. Then the next group. Step back. Next. Step back. When the space is 80 percent full, stop.

If you think of decluttering only as what you're getting rid of, you'll begin to feel anxious and may come to a grinding halt.

No one likes to feel like things are being taken away from them.

It's like when you're on a diet and you think only about the things you can't eat. It messes with your head. But when you think about all of the yummy things that do fit into your plan, you feel more satisfied.

For example:

STEP 1: Pull all your shoes out (that includes any by the front door, in the mudroom, next to the treadmill, or anywhere else in the house).

STEP 2: Do a quick run-through of your first layers of trash, broken items, and unused items. Shoes with dust on them, holes in them, or detached soles, go.

STEP 3: Pick up each remaining pair, one by one.

STEP 4: Ask yourself if you're keeping the ones in your hand.

STEP 5: Build your keep and donate piles.

STEP 6: When you've gotten through them all, remove the donate pile from the room.

STEP 7: Mindfully place the keepers back in their home.

Now you can see all the shoes you have, love, and wear.

THE REST GOES BUH-BYE

If something isn't a keeper, then it needs to go. When it goes, you'll feel lighter. The crap you collect around your house that you don't want, need, or use weighs you down.

Do not let bags and boxes of donations and other to-go categories pile up in your house, garage, basement, or shed. Put them in your car, or by the front door if you've scheduled a pickup. I have story after story of people who didn't have a plan to remove the boxes or bags, and they sat there for months, even years, because they became white noise that everyone just worked around.

Don't let to-go stuff become a new kind of clutter.

PASSING THINGS ON

If you want to give something to someone, like a memento of a deceased loved one, take that item to that person, put it in a box and ship it, or have them come over ASAP to pick it up. Just make sure you're not passing things on in a way that turns your clutter into someone else's, please.

DONATIONS

This is the most popular option, so if you can pop everything in your car and run it over to a donation center today, do it. If you want to donate to specific places like women's shelters or animal shelters, make a plan to take them there this week. No excuses!

SELLING

A friend of mine made $10,000 on eBay when she downsized and decluttered her home. Selling is a great option if you have the energy and resources.

I donate everything that doesn't get tossed because I do

not have the energy to go through the steps of selling my stuff.

Places like eBay, consignment shops, Poshmark, and other small businesses in your area that resell items can help with this process if you want to sell some things. Consider using the money you make for a vacation, new organizational stuff, or to pay off debt, instead of bringing more crap into your home.

RECYCLING/UPCYCLING

If you don't have people in your life you'd want to pass things on to, don't have items the local shelters want, don't love the idea of donating to big-box donation centers like Goodwill, or don't have the energy or time to sell your stuff, and maybe are looking for options that feel Earth-friendly, you can consider ideas like textile or metal recycling—the availability of which varies by area, so do your research—Buy Nothing Project groups on Facebook or online at buynothingproject.org, or The Freecycle Network at freecycle.org.

You have lots of options. Don't get overwhelmed. There's no wrong choice here, just the choice that's right for you.

THE TAKEAWAY

When you remove all of the mental shit, decluttering is a basic step-by-step process. You may have been thinking something was wrong with you because you've read so many step-by-step processes that seemed so logical, yet somehow you couldn't get the job done.

There has never been anything wrong with you.

You needed to understand the emotion side of things so you could find that balance between the logic and the emotion.

Now you have that, plus you have your basic steps to fall back on as you move forward. It's time to start putting this all into action!

MAKING IT REAL

When you've completed a section, a room, or the whole damn thing, you can look back on how you answered these questions and see if you kept the things you loved or if they changed, and see if you attended to the things you hated.

HOME RELATIONSHIP ASSESSMENT

What do you love about your home, room by room?

Kitchen	Family Room	Living Room
Primary Bedroom	Guest Room	Kids' Room #1
Kids' Room #2	Dining Room	Primary Bath
Half Bath #1	Half Bath #2	Full Bath
Laundry Room	Playroom	Office
Garage	Attic	Basement
Storage Shed	Yard	Exercise Room
Entryway	Mudroom	Sunroom
Other	Other	Other

What do you dislike about your home, room by room?

Kitchen	Family Room	Living Room
Primary Bedroom	Guest Room	Kids' Room #1
Kids' Room #2	Dining Room	Primary Bath
Half Bath #1	Half Bath #2	Full Bath
Laundry Room	Playroom	Office
Garage	Attic	Basement
Storage Shed	Yard	Exercise Room
Entryway	Mudroom	Sunroom
Other	Other	Other

Before you start on your home, answer these questions. They will be repeated at the end of each chapter in Part 2, but for now answer them as they pertain to your house as a whole:	
What do you feel when you think about decluttering your home? Check all that apply: ☐ **Angry** ☐ **Hopeless** ☐ **Anxious** ☐ **Joyful** ☐ **Ashamed** ☐ **Loving** ☐ **Doubtful** ☐ **Overwhelmed** ☐ **Excited** ☐ **Sad** ☐ **Hopeful** ☐ **Other** ________	How would you like to feel about your home? Please describe:
What Stage of Change do you see yourself in when you think about your home? (*See Chapter 1.*) Why?	If you haven't reached Action, what do you think you need to do to move into the next stage? (*See Chapter 1.*)
What limiting beliefs have kept you from decluttering your home? (*See Chapter 2.*)	What fears do you have about beginning to declutter your home? (*See Chapter 2.*)
If you are feeling shame, describe what about your home makes you feel there is something wrong with you. (*See Chapter 3.*)	If you are dealing with perfectionism, how is that holding you back from taking care of your home? (*See Chapter 3.*)
How are your values either shown or attacked in your home? (*See Chapter 4.*)	What habits have led to the clutter in your home? (*See Chapter 5.*)
What are your top five goals for your home? (*See Chapter 6.*) **1.** **2.** **3.** **4.** **5.**	What steps will you take to reach those goals? (*See Chapter 6.*) **1.** **2.** **3.** **4.** **5.**

CHAPTER 8

HOLY SHIT, IS THAT A SLAP CHOP?

Let's get started with the heart of your home: the kitchen.

My own decluttering journey went from an idea I was messing around with to a plan I was dedicated to in the kitchen. It's a common place to start decluttering because it's used so much that it can become messy and cluttered almost as fast as you can clean and tidy it.

We tend to feel best when preparing meals in a tidy, organized space, so it's natural to want to clean it up and out.

MY BREAKING POINT

We have an eat-in kitchen that is one big room at the back of the house adjacent to the family room. At dinner we sit at the table, my hubby facing into the family room, looking at the big-ass TV (which I insisted on buying, not him). I sit kitty-corner from him, facing the kitchen counters.

On this particular evening, with a lovely, comforting dinner that he made for us, I was hunched over my plate, staring at the crap and mess all around me.

I had shoved the mail and various other shit to one end of the table so we could put plates on our placemats to eat "like civilized people," as we call it. Otherwise, we eat sitting on the couch, which I kind of prefer because I don't really like chairs. They're so stiff and unyielding, and I'm like a cat: I want to curl up and snuggle in all the time.

But I digress. The kitchen counter was also covered in crap. Dirty dishes, supplements, kitchen gadgets, cleaning supplies, bowls of hot sauce and ketchup packets, bottles of water-flavoring concentrates, even fortune cookies. Seriously, when I say crap, I mean *crap*.

This is not to mention the kitchen sink, which was not just filled with that day's dishes. Oh no, there were dishes that had been there for at least a week.

You see, Shawn does most of the cooking in our house and I do the dishes. It's a pretty good deal. However, I used to habitually let the dishes pile up in the sink until it was unbearable, either the sight or the stench, and then I would finally do a load of dishes. But after waiting so long, there were inevitably too many dishes to fit in the dishwasher, so some would end up staying in the sink. I'd rinse them off to get rid of the smell—I'm not an animal, you know—and then they would be the foundation for the next pile. What the actual fuck!?

☆ SUCCESS STRATEGY ☆

Whether you do it first thing in the morning or right before bed, always do the dishes and wipe down the counters.

My sweet, patient hubby looked at me, as I glowered and grumbled to myself like a dissatisfied vulture, and asked what was wrong. I burst out with a growling "I hate all this fucking shit!"

Wise man that he is, he said a cautious "Okay . . ." and returned to his meal.

That was when the dam broke. I hated my home. I hated everything I saw. I hate to admit it, but I think I hated me.

I was disgusted and horrified and dragged down by the clutter and disorganization. This situation had to change. I was tired of the way it looked and how it made me feel.

That moment launched me into the three-month decluttering and organizing frenzy I refer to as the "Great Decluttering" that changed my entire life.

THINGS THAT MAKE YOU GO HMMM . . .

WHAT STYLE OF ORGANIZATION IS BEST FOR YOUR PERSONALITY?

There are those who enjoy Visual Abundance and those who prefer Visual Simplicity. I first came across this idea during the Great Decluttering, and it helped me understand why my organization hadn't been working, and what to change.

Professional organizer Cassandra Aarssen shares what her experiences as an organizer taught her about different types of organizing personalities in her book *Clutterbug*. Here, I'm sharing her concepts of Visual and Organizational Abundance and Simplicity because I've found it helpful for my clients to use as a foundation when attacking organizing tasks like pantries and cabinets.

Visual Abundance: When you prefer to use clear or wire containers so you can see what is in them. You like to have things out on countertops so you don't forget they exist.

Visual Simplicity: When you prefer solid containers like baskets and opaque plastic or cloth bins. You feel most at peace when there is next to nothing on countertops and tables.

Organizational Abundance: When you like to have things organized into lots of smaller bins, boxes, jars, etc. You feel like you can find things better if they're separated out into individual labeled containers.

Organizational Simplicity: When you prefer to have large bins or containers that hold larger categories of items. You like the ability to toss things into larger labeled bins instead of messing with tiny details.

As with all personality types and styles, no one is 100 percent anything. I'm a visual-simplicity kind of gal, but I have all of my daily protein, collagen, magnesium powder, pre-workout powder, and biotin gummies and pill case out so I don't forget they exist. Middle-path solution? Clean white containers for everything so they reduce the visual noise.

WELL, SHIT, AM I READY FOR THIS?

Because you spend so much time either in your kitchen or avoiding your kitchen, it might feel like you should be ready to start here.

But you may or may not actually be there yet.

Let's sort this shit out, and look at what each Stage of Change (*see Chapter 1*) might look like in your kitchen:

- **Precontemplation:** "I don't see the issue. I can find food and dishes when needed, so why bother?"
- **Contemplation:** "Yup, this sucks. Damn, I wish I could get myself motivated so I don't have to look at those dishes and all that crap on the counters every day."
- **Preparation:** "Okay, that's it! I refuse to keep feeling like something is going to attack me every time I open a cupboard or walk into the pantry."
- **Action:** "Holy crap, how did we end up with five garlic presses? Four of you are leaving today!"
- **Maintenance:** "My kitchen is under control and, as long as I stay on top of it, nothing grows in the fridge, and the counters stay clear, I'm a happy camper."

What do you think?

- Is the kitchen the least of your worries?
- Is it beginning to get on your nerves?
- Are you pulling out a pen and paper while reading this to write down your plan? (Nice multitasking, if so, BTW.)

- Are you reading this while packing up dishes to be donated?
- Or are you feeling pretty good because you've already dealt with your kitchen and are in the maintain-and-hone stage?

SHITTY THINKING IN YOUR KITCHEN

Because your kitchen is so in your face, it can trigger a lot of crappy thoughts that make you want to turn around and run. That's totally normal!

But before you run, do me a favor and think about what your thoughts might be that are making the kitchen feel so damn overwhelming.

Limiting Beliefs: Whether you were raised in a house with a pristine kitchen where dinners were made every day or a house with mold in the fridge and everyone fended for themselves, you got some messages about yourself and what you're capable of.

You may be looking around thinking:

- "I'm too lazy to stay on top of my kitchen like other people."
- "I've always had a hard time keeping on top of the dishes—that's just how I am."
- "I've organized that pantry a hundred times, and it always returns to chaos. Clearly I suck at this."

A kitchen is just a room full of a lot of crap that gets used and moved around over and over again.

How about you switch it up to:

- "I haven't kept a kitchen tidy yet, but I've also never tried it like this before."
- "Dishes are a pain in the ass for everyone. I wasn't born with a defective dish-washing gene."
- "Oh, I get it! The way I've been organizing the pantry hasn't been working, so I need to find a system that *does* work."

> **SUCCESS STRATEGY**
>
> **Be honest with yourself about the stuff you have. If you got a bunch of fancy utensils for your wedding that you've never used, it's time to release them into the wild.**

Fears: Limiting beliefs run hand in hand with fear, so let's look at what is so damn scary about your kitchen that you keep turning a blind eye to it.

If you declutter and organize your kitchen, are you afraid:

- You'll get rid of too many pots and be in trouble next Thanksgiving?
- Your family will get mad at you for moving the potato chips to a different place in the pantry?
- You'll be expected to cook more?
- Other people will think you should have put the kitchen gadgets in a different drawer and the coffee mugs closer to the stove?

Whatever the fear, you have to decide if it's worth facing. Will having a kitchen you feel proud of be worth the risk? Only you can tell.

LETTING GO OF SOME SHIT

All those fears can leave you feeling ashamed of yourself and your kitchen, worried you won't do it "right." We base a lot of our self-worth on the state of our kitchens, so it's easy to torture yourself with perfectionism.

Not only is the kitchen the place you feed your family, it's also where people congregate when they come over, right? Not the living room you fluffed and vacuumed just special for them, but the kitchen where things are baking, boiling, chilling, and generally making a mess.

It's the one room you just *know* people are judging you on the cleanliness of.

That judgment you're so sure is happening (and hey, maybe it is, maybe it isn't) is what tells you that you should feel shame over the state of your kitchen.

It's time to manage your expectations. When you go over to someone else's house, they probably just spent hours making it look "right" for you too. Try not to make up crappier rules for yourself than you have for everyone else.

Perfectionism: Our culture puts a lot of expectations on us to have a Betty Crocker-worthy kitchen at all times. Look, you *live* in your house.

- ✕ Grease sticks to the cabinets.
- ✕ Dishes are never really done, even if you do them every damn day.
- ✕ Someone always leaves the peanut butter sitting out on the counter.
- ✕ And which kid has those "yogurt hands" and keeps touching things!?

Get real with yourself.
There is no such thing as a perfect kitchen.

There is a tidy kitchen, an organized kitchen, and a functional kitchen. Accept the cycle of use in your kitchen and let yourself off the hook for once.

☆ SUCCESS STRATEGY ☆

Be sure to mindfully individualize your systems so they work for you and your lifestyle.

Shame: So, you decide to take a huge step in facing shame and you invite people over. You're letting people in, which, if you haven't decluttered and created systems yet, may mean you're shoving stuff into closets and under beds, to stage it as best you can.

You're being brave and letting them in, but you're still afraid they:

- ✕ Judge you for not having enough clear counter space.
- ✕ Gag at the gunk in the sink strainer.
- ✕ Tsk-tsk at the chaos hiding in your cabinets when they start fishing around for a platter for the veggie tray they brought.

But if you want to be able to enjoy entertaining, let alone using your kitchen on a daily basis, it's time to own and accept yourself and your kitchen. This is *your* kitchen. Make it work for you, and the people who are worth a ticket to your party won't care one way or the other.

THE SHIT YOU VALUE

When I think about how my own kitchen used to not fit my value system, I think about my values of:

- Health—and how an ever-present mound of dishes, complete with slime and gunk, was totally counter to that value.
- Not wasting food—despite all the veggies that had gone bad in the fridge and canned goods that went out of date five years ago.
- Intentional living—and how hard it was to uphold when my kitchen was such a hot mess and meal-planning was out of the question.

☆ SUCCESS STRATEGY ☆

Use a black Magic Marker to write the date you purchased items on them so you can be sure to rotate your stock to use the oldest first.

Some of your own values may look like:

- Feeding your family in a sanitary space.
- Being able to make meals in a timely manner to keep life rolling.
- Knowing what you have in your fridge and pantry so you don't waste money rebuying things you already have.

Are your values represented in your kitchen? If not, are you ready to do something about it?

THINGS THAT MAKE YOU GO HMMM . . .

One of my values is the use of nontoxic cleaning products. I've pulled together some of my favorite recipes to make your own cleaning solutions that are nontoxic, easy, and less expensive than what you'll get at the store.

PRODUCT	INGREDIENTS	INSTRUCTIONS
ALL-PURPOSE CLEANER	16 oz dark glass spray bottle A spoonful of white vinegar Distilled water 40 drops of essential oils ***Recommendations:*** Lemon, any other citrus oils, tea tree, peppermint	Combine these ingredients in your bottle. Label it. Shake it. Spray it.
HAND SOAP	Dark glass bottle with pump; size of your choice Unscented castile soap Essential oils ***Recommendations:*** Antiseptic oils like lemon, tea tree, juniper berry, and grapefruit Anti-infection oils like lavender, tea tree, ylang ylang, and geranium	Use a 1–2 percent dilution rate. ***For example:*** 8 oz castile soap with 40–80 drops total of oils Combine and you're ready to go!
WOOD POLISH	16 oz dark glass spray bottle ½ cup olive oil ½ cup white vinegar 20 drops of essential oils ***Recommendations:*** Lemon, orange, arborvitae, lavender, tea tree	Combine these ingredients in your bottle. Label it. Shake it. Spray it.
FLOOR CLEANER	¼ cup vinegar 1 gallon hot water 2 tablespoons castile soap Approximately 15–20 drops of eucalyptus and peppermint essential oils Or you can try a milder, more child-friendly scent of 10–20 drops of a citrus oil or blend.	Combine everything in a large bucket and clean your floor as usual.
SOFT SCRUBBING CLEANSER	¾ cup baking soda ¼ cup castile soap 1 tablespoon water 10 drops lemon or orange essential oil	Add all ingredients to a Mason jar and mix well. Use half of a real lemon to increase the acidity for greater cleansing. Use a melamine foam sponge (aka Mr. Clean Magic Eraser) for even more oomph.

GETTING OVER YOUR SHITTY HABITS

The habits you have are what decide whether your kitchen is functional or a hazard zone. If it tends to lean toward hazardous, you're probably feeling a ton of shame over the things you keep doing, making it hard for you to shake it off and reset crappy habits like:

- Putting dishes in the sink instead of the dishwasher.
- Tossing things into drawers and cabinets willy-nilly.
- Dropping crap like mail, book bags, keys, permission slips, etc. on the kitchen table or counters.

> ☆ SUCCESS STRATEGY ☆
>
> **If it will take less than sixty seconds, do it now.**

If you have a limiting belief like "Before and after school is too rushed, I don't have time to keep up with the kitchen," you'll keep falling back onto habits that don't match your values, and the shame spiral over your hazard zone will keep going.

> ☆ SUCCESS STRATEGY ☆
>
> **Keep plastic utensils, cups, and plates (check out compostable options) on hand for those days when you simply can't face doing the dishes.**

LET'S SET THE SHIT OUT OF SOME GOALS

If you're ready to do something about your kitchen situation, you must be in Preparation. Congratulations!

It's time to set some goals. Where do you want to start?

- **Small Victory:** Clearing out one drawer.
- **Big Impact:** Getting rid of that extra CrockPot that's been taking up space on your counter even though it's broken.
- **Irritant:** Clearing out under the sink so you can finally fit all of your cleaning supplies under there instead of having them clutter up the counter-top.
- **Worst:** Emptying and cleaning out the refrigerator.

Wherever you start, make sure it makes sense to you. Make your plan. Be honest and realistic about time.

- You may be short on time and energy, so the pantry and fridge might be a bit much to ask of yourself in one day.
- You might have twelve hours to dedicate to tearing this bitch down and putting her back together.
- You may need to keep it simple and do one drawer, one cabinet, or one shelf per day.

THE TAKEAWAY

Remember, you're the one who has to work and live in this kitchen. Declutter and organize in a way that makes sense to your life. If you're a frozen meal kinda gal, you don't need to have every kitchen gadget on the planet. If you love to cook, you'll want to have a clear space and systems that make it easy to clean when you're done.

Bon appétit!

MAKING IT REAL

Now that you've worked on yourself, and you've thought about how the Mental Shit impacts the Physical Shit, let's put your newfound knowledge and thinking into practice.

Before you declutter your kitchen, answer these questions.

What do you feel when you think about decluttering your kitchen? Check all that apply: ☐ **Angry** ☐ **Hopeless** ☐ **Anxious** ☐ **Joyful** ☐ **Ashamed** ☐ **Loving** ☐ **Doubtful** ☐ **Overwhelmed** ☐ **Excited** ☐ **Sad** ☐ **Hopeful** ☐ **Other** ________	How would you like to feel about your kitchen? Please describe:
What Stage of Change do you see yourself in when you think about your kitchen? (*See Chapter 1.*) Why?	If you haven't reached Action, what do you think you need to do to move into the next stage? (*See Chapter 1.*)
What limiting beliefs have kept you from decluttering your kitchen? (*See Chapter 2.*)	What fears do you have about beginning to declutter your kitchen? (*See Chapter 2.*)
If you are feeling shame, describe what about your kitchen makes you feel there is something wrong with you. (*See Chapter 3.*)	If you are dealing with perfectionism, how is that holding you back from taking care of your kitchen? (*See Chapter 3.*)
How are your values either shown or attacked in your kitchen? (*See Chapter 4.*)	What habits have led to the clutter in your kitchen? (*See Chapter 5.*)
What are your top five goals for your kitchen? (*See Chapter 6.*) **1.** **2.** **3.** **4.** **5.**	What steps will you take to reach those goals? (*See Chapter 6.*) **1.** **2.** **3.** **4.** **5.**

KITCHEN CHECKLIST

☐ Old spices	☐ Lidless containers	☐ Cleaning supplies	☐ Candles
☐ Expired food	☐ Containerless lids	☐ Dish towels/rags	☐ Aprons
☐ Duplicate items	☐ Coffee cups	☐ Old sponges	☐ Tablecloths
☐ Unused gadgets	☐ Souvenir anything	☐ Outgrown kid stuff	☐ ________
☐ Takeout menus	☐ Cookbooks	☐ Magnets	☐ ________
☐ Chipped dishes	☐ Ugly decor	☐ Junk drawer	☐ ________

After you've decluttered your kitchen, come back and answer these questions.

How do you feel when you think about your kitchen now?

What new habits will you be putting in place to maintain your kitchen?

Do you have any new goals for your kitchen since decluttering?

CHAPTER 9

CALGON, TAKE THIS SHIT AWAY

Bathrooms are one of the top things homebuyers look at, and yet once you move in, the bathroom becomes a forgotten and overlooked space you rush in and out of for various personal reasons.

But a bathroom is so much more than that. Did you know that Feng Shui teaches us to put the toilet lid down before you flush? Otherwise, wealth energy goes swirling down and out of your house. It's like energetically flushing away money.

Did you also know that you need to keep that lid down because every time you flush, the toilet spray from whatever was in there shoots straight up? Ew. Gross.

Bathrooms are where you clean yourself, yet they're more prone to poor sanitation than any other room in your house.

When guests come over, you make damn sure you've scrubbed that downstairs bathroom and pray to all that is holy that no one takes it upon themselves to use the upstairs bathroom with all the products and towels everywhere.

Decluttering will make it easier to create systems to keep all of your bathrooms orderly, or at least require no more than a quick wipedown and tidy-up in a guest emergency.

I have two bathrooms: a full bath upstairs, and a half bath downstairs. Most of my guests keep to the first floor. But on any given day, I'm okay with someone using the upstairs bathroom. There's rarely anything on the sink, everything is tucked away, towels are hung up because there are more than enough hooks, and even the kitty litter is tidied up every day.

Decluttered. Organized. Functional. Beautiful. These are the words I want you to keep in mind when you think about your bathrooms.

THE FORGOTTEN ROOM

My bathrooms, all one and a half of them, were the first rooms to get taken down to the studs and redesigned. There's something about a fresh, clean bathroom that makes you feel good.

The funny thing was the difference in how each of them got done. The full bath was done before I decluttered the house. The half bath was done after I decluttered.

The full bath is nice. I really like the floor tiles and the nook in the shower. But since I did the half bath, which is now my favorite room in my house, I want a redo on the full bath.

Before decluttering, I was a hot mess inside, so was totally overwhelmed and unsure of myself in making decisions. After decluttering, I felt confident and focused, with a clear vision and plan.

When I did declutter and reorganize those bathrooms, it was a lot of "Why do we have this?" and "How old is this?" and "Dear Lord, more towels?" Thankfully, I didn't run into a lot of "Eww!" But I know people who have.

One client, Colleen, sat down on her bathroom floor and took a full hour to declutter, wipe down, and replace items under the sink. That's not a lot of space, but damn! You can hide a lot of crap in there.

And it tends to be stuff you've totally forgotten you had. Colleen told me she found shampoo she didn't even remember buying. She found cleaning supplies still in the packaging.

That was all before she hit her linen closet. She was under strict orders (by me) to take their everyday bath towels down to two per household person, plus two for the rare event of an overnight guest. She practically emptied her linen closet. The local animal shelter got one hell of a gift that day.

> ☆ **SUCCESS STRATEGY** ☆
>
> **Lean into the two-towels-per-person rule. This does not include beach towels. Yes, you do laundry more often, but is that really a bad thing?**

Then there were the medications. Colleen had been an EMT and a firefighter, so was all about preparedness. This led to keeping every prescription she, her husband, and her son ever got. The bin she kept them in was bursting at the seams. The criterion of not being out of date took that down by half, and a new system of organization was implemented for daily-use medications and what she calls the "zombie apocalypse" medications—things like unused, but still in date, antibiotics, steroids, etc.

Oh, yeah, and then what about her cosmetics? This was a woman who rarely wore makeup, but when she did, she did it up. I believe she experienced physical pain when getting rid of expired eye shadows, even though all of her medical training told her it was the logical, sanitary thing to do.

> ☆ SUCCESS STRATEGY ☆
>
> **As soon as you open a product, write the date (or the period after opening, your choice) on the container. Now you know when to toss it!**

In the end, the one bathroom shared by three people was clean and orderly in a way it could be maintained, which saved a ton of time for everyone.

Colleen was ready for Action, but she hadn't started there. She had worked to get herself there, just like you're going to.

WELL, SHIT, AM I READY FOR THIS?

Colleen's story is one I've seen over and over. She went from Contemplation, to Preparation, to Action in about one day. It was like she couldn't unsee the chaos in there once she truly looked at it through my eyes.

So, where are you at?

- ✕ **Precontemplation:** "It's fine the way it is. I see no problem with the walls of the shower being green." (FYI, this is the true story of a house I moved into for a summer during college. Boys had been living there, and I couldn't take a shower until I had cleaned it, turning it from green to white. "Huh, I didn't even notice that" was the response my male friends gave me. Seriously. They were in Precontemplation, I was in Action.)

- **Contemplation:** "I know the bathroom needs work, but I don't have time to go digging through closets and under sinks."
- **Preparation:** "Okay, this is bad. I can't take a shower in here until something is done about it. Rubber gloves and a lot of bleach are going to be needed."
- **Action:** "Holy heck, how do we have cold medicine that expired ten years ago? In the bin you go!"
- **Maintenance:** "The one room I can get away from my kids in (usually) finally feels like the oasis I needed."

What do you think?

- Is the bathroom fine as it is?
- Are you starting to notice more and more things you would want to change?
- Are you detailing your plan of attack?
- Is the attack in full swing?
- Do you already have your oasis, and are reveling in it?

Wherever you are, think about what you would need to move you into the next stage.

THINGS THAT MAKE YOU GO HMMM . . .

WHAT!? NOW I HAVE TO TOSS MY MAKEUP TOO?

Did you know your makeup, skin care, and hair care all have expiration dates? Liquids will break down over time, whether you opened the product or not. You can usually tell when you try to use them that something is wrong. Other products begin to break down as soon as you open them and touch them. This is one way a well-curated and decluttered bathroom will save you hundreds of dollars.

A few issues that old products will have are:

Liquids separate.

Anything a brush touches is covered in bacteria.

Effectiveness of key ingredients wears off.

Period after opening dates for cosmetics:

Concealer: One year

Cream blush: One year

Eyeliner: Three months

Eyeliner pencil: Two years

Eye shadow: One year

Foundation: One year

Lip balm: One to five years

Lip gloss: One year

Lipstick: Two years

Liquid eyeliner: Three months

Mascara: Three months

Nail polish: One year

Powder blush: Two years

Expiration dates for skin and hair care:

Bar soap: Eighteen months to three years

Bath oil: One year

Bleaches and depilatories: Six months

Body lotion: Two years

Body wash: Three years

Conditioner: Two to three years

Deodorant: One to two years

Eye cream: One year

Face cream: Two years

Hair gel: Two to three years

Hair spray: Two to three years

Loofah: Six months

Makeup sponge: One month

Shampoo: Two to three years

Miscellaneous expiration periods:

Mouthwash: Three years from the manufacture date

Nail polish remover: Indefinitely

Perfume: One to two years

Shaving cream: Two years

Sunscreen: Three years

Toothbrush: Three months

Toothpaste: Two years

SHITTY THINKING IN YOUR BATHROOM

Are you thinking, "It's a bathroom. What could she possibly think my limiting beliefs and fears are in this little room?" If so, I totally get it. The bathroom doesn't seem like a terribly triggering room. And yet, you still haven't decluttered it. Hmm, there must be something going on.

Limiting Beliefs: Your limiting beliefs may be more about not having enough time to get to it.

No matter how busy your life is, if something is important enough, you'll make the time.

This poor underappreciated, forgotten space where old shower gel goes to die might feel like the last of your worries. The limiting belief could be that it isn't as important as other rooms.

All I can say to this is that I know you'll feel amazing when you declutter your bathroom and there is organization under the sink and in the medicine cabinets because you took the time and prioritized a space you use repeatedly throughout every day.

Fears: The bathroom is a scary room for many people. You have to use it, but you don't have to like it. Often this is because it's the one place you get naked in that has a big-ass mirror in it. If you don't like the way you look or don't like your body, the bathroom can be a room you spend as little time in as possible.

Of course, there are those who spend a lot of time in the bathroom, reading, watching movies, playing video games, contemplating life, etc., but they clearly do not fit in our current category of fear.

Bathrooms can also feel connected to illness, as they are where you head to when you have something like a stomach virus (or perhaps indulged a wee bit too much), which ain't pretty to start with, plus many people have phobias around vomiting. Bathrooms are also where we tend to keep first-aid supplies for incidents like when I dropped a large, sharp piece of metal on my foot (on my birthday, no less) and was bleeding all over the house before I realized how bad it was and got myself to the bathroom where Shawn calmly took matters in hand and wrapped it up. Turns out the damn thing was actually fractured, happy birthday to me!

But on the day-to-day, your bathroom is a room dedicated to self-care, which can feel intimidating if you tend to whip past self-care on the regular.

To care for yourself, you have to like yourself.

If you don't like yourself all that much, a self-care room can be scary.

The premise of this book is based on the idea that caring for your home is self-care. Well, caring for your bathroom is *really* looking self-care dead in the face. So if you'd prefer to ignore and avoid, you won't want to deal with this room.

Maybe a spa day for you is a day when you face your fear of your own body and care for the room you care for your body in.

LETTING GO OF SOME SHIT

You have not failed at life if you have a bathroom in disrepair. Failure is the fear of every perfectionist. Failure conjures up shame like nothing else.

Perfectionism: Bathrooms are a place your guests are definitely going to go. You want the room to be pristine, tidy, and attractive if possible. Once you begin to dig into a bathroom, you unearth a lot of stuff. This becomes overwhelming when you expect perfection, because your mindset will likely be that once you start something, you can't stop.

"What if I start going through all of my expired prescriptions and run out of time?" The simple answer is you'll get back to it.

But the perfectionist doesn't want to hear that. The perfectionist wants to have a beginning, middle, and end, and anything less is unacceptable.

If this sounds like you, it's time to rethink what your expectations are of yourself, because they're probably keeping you from getting shit done.

Shame: If you don't like your bathroom, you might be turning a blind eye to it, leaving yourself feeling embarrassed when people come over.

I hated our old bathrooms with their builder-grade everything. And the half bath smelled. I could not figure out and never did figure out what it was. Taking it down to the studs was the only thing that made the smell go away.

It was embarrassing to have guests use that bathroom. Maybe they didn't notice the smell or the ugly vanity and mirror, but I did.

When we remodeled our upstairs bathroom, guests invited themselves up there to see it. They didn't do that when we repainted and redecorated the bedroom (which I love, by the way, and would like to show off).

Now my favorite room in my house is my downstairs half bath, which we remodeled a couple of years later. I glow every time someone tells me how nice it is. Glow.

Decluttering those rooms has allowed me to be proud of these spaces I know my guests will be using, instead of a little cringy. The work was well worth it.

THE SHIT YOU VALUE

Cleanliness is next to...whatever entity you look to for guidance. In our culture, sanitation and cleanliness are held in very high regard. So it's likely, regardless of what your bathroom looks like, that you value these things. If you don't have them, you're living contrary to your own values.

Tara, a client who was a highly paid executive, lived in a tiny house overridden by clutter. Cleanliness was of very high value to her.

She showered daily but was doing it in a room that was about six feet by eight feet, overrun with clutter and mayhem.

The shower didn't drain properly, the sink didn't even work due to a broken pipe, and every surface was covered in hair products, shaving paraphernalia, and everything else you might find in a bathroom. Yet the medicine cabinet was empty.

She is actually one of my favorite clients; she made one of the most amazing life changes I've ever seen. When we first met, she had a severe anxiety disorder that led to lying, and hiding things out of shame, then getting caught up by those lies. She was caught in a vicious circle that caused regular panic attacks. Today she lives by her values of honesty and health.

She has lost weight, she is amazed at how strong she is, she eats mindfully, she has work boundaries, and, get this, she has literally demolished the house that had gotten so decayed by lack of care that it made more sense to start over again.

In the new house, Tara is taking the opportunity to reset her lifestyle to fit her values and to include healthier habits. She is excited to have bathrooms that are not only attractive, but also set up with systems that are maintainable for organization and sanitation.

When I first met Tara, she didn't believe she deserved these things. Now she knows she does, and she's making damn sure she gets them and keeps them.

THINGS THAT MAKE YOU GO HMMM . . .

WHAT DO I DO WITH ALL OF THE EXPIRED PRESCRIPTIONS IN MY MEDICINE CABINET?

Over-the-counter medications and prescription medications all have expiration dates. The expiration is based on the expectation of how long a medication is at full potency.

So, hoarding all those old meds isn't actually doing you any good. If they're expired and you actually take them, you may be sorely disappointed in their effectiveness. Instead, get rid of them!

Now, what do you do with these expired medications? Toss them? What about if a child or animal finds them and eats them? Flush them? Isn't that poisoning the water table?

I got you, boo. Here are some options.

1. Drop them off at or mail them to a drug take-back site. You can look online or talk to your pharmacy or local police department to find one.

2. The Food and Drug Administration has a Flush List that you can find at FDA.gov. This is a list of drugs that would be dangerous to be found and ingested, so they recommend flushing them.

3. If the medications you have are not on the Flush List or you don't like the idea of sending potential toxins into the water supply, these are the FDA's recommendations for putting them in the trash:

   Mix medicines (liquid or pills; do not crush tablets or capsules) with an unappealing substance such as dirt, cat litter, or used coffee grounds.

   Place the mixture in a container such as a sealed plastic bag.

   Throw away the container in your trash at home.

   Delete all personal information on the prescription label of empty medicine bottles or medicine packaging, then trash or recycle the empty bottle or packaging.

GETTING OVER YOUR SHITTY HABITS

Shitty habits in the bathroom sounds inappropriate—or really funny, depending on your mood.

Bathrooms get fucked up right quick because of some of those terrible habits.

- ✕ Not replacing the toilet paper roll (personal pet peeve).
- ✕ Tossing makeup into a drawer with no system in place.
- ✕ Buying soap and shampoo whether you need it or not.
- ✕ Keeping old towels when you get new ones "just in case."
- ✕ Keeping expired medications.
- ✕ Letting makeup powder get all over everything.
- ✕ Tossing things under the sink willy-nilly because it's easy.
- ✕ Leaving the shaving cream out.
- ✕ Not wiping down the sink when you get toothpaste all over it.
- ✕ Getting baby powder all over the place when you powder your bum.
- ✕ Not putting the toilet lid down (we talked about this already).

I kinda feel like I could go on and on here. This is the "rush in, do what you gotta do, rush out" room. Well, unless you're a sit and contemplate for forty-five minutes on the toilet kind of person. But even then, do you put the magazine you were reading back in the magazine holder, or leave it on the sink?

☆ SUCCESS STRATEGY ☆

Make things as simple as possible for everyone in your family to keep the bathrooms tidy. Have there be as few steps as you can for them to follow the new systems.

After you declutter a bathroom, it gets really easy to keep it that way if you have the right systems in place. When I designed our bathrooms, I kept in mind the replacing-of-the-toilet-roll issue and got pivoting toilet-roll holders. They take about three steps out of replacing the roll. After further observation of our half bath in particular, I realized I needed to make it even simpler to get to the toilet-paper roll to replace it and set up a basket on the back of the toilet with extra rolls within easy reach. We now have about a 98 percent success rate of roll replacement in that bathroom. I'm pretty sure I'm a genius.

Observe yourself and your family. Figure out what shitty habits are happening and why. Use those observations to help you create new goals to focus on.

LET'S SET THE SHIT OUT OF SOME GOALS

All-righty, you've gotten this far, and you're ready to get goal-oriented in the bathroom. What's that going to look like?

- **Small Victory:** Toss all of your clumpy old nail polish.
- **Big Impact:** Get rid of all but two towels per person.
- **Irritant:** Go through all of your OTC medications and get rid of out-of-date stuff so you aren't having to make

midnight runs to the store for the right stuff because you know what you have.

- **Worst:** Dig into the deep, dark recesses of the vanity under the sink.

If you have more than one bathroom, you'll want to divide your goals up between all of them.

I recommend finishing one before going on to the next. When you spread it out, it's easy to get distracted or forget what's been done where.

When you're in each bathroom, divide it up into sections. Maybe you can get an entire half bath done in one quick go, but a primary bath or kids' bathroom may take a little more dividing.

Decide if you're dividing by category or by section.

- Is it cosmetics, skin care, hair care, towels, medicines, etc.?
- Or under the sink, the shower, the shelves in the linen closet, the medicine cabinet, etc.?

As always, be realistic and time-conscious. Don't bite off more than you can chew, or else you'll run out of steam and risk never finishing.

THE TAKEAWAY

Whether you have one bathroom or five, each one needs love and attention. You can have all your bathrooms be guest-ready with decluttering and organizing. No shame required.

When you believe you deserve to have little oases in your home, you'll dig in. Who knows, maybe you'll be like me and get more compliments on your half bath than anything else in your house!

MAKING IT REAL

Now that you've worked on yourself, and you've reviewed the process of decluttering your bathroom, it's time to check in, get honest, and create a plan.

Before you declutter your bathroom, answer these questions:

What do you feel when you think about decluttering your bathroom? Check all that apply: ☐ **Angry** ☐ **Hopeless** ☐ **Anxious** ☐ **Joyful** ☐ **Ashamed** ☐ **Loving** ☐ **Doubtful** ☐ **Overwhelmed** ☐ **Excited** ☐ **Sad** ☐ **Hopeful** ☐ **Other** ________	How would you like to feel about your bathroom? Please describe:
What Stage of Change do you see yourself in when you think about your bathroom? (*See Chapter 1.*) Why?	If you haven't reached Action, what do you think you need to do to move into the next stage? (*See Chapter 1.*)
What limiting beliefs have kept you from decluttering your bathroom? (*See Chapter 2.*)	What fears do you have about beginning to declutter your bathroom? (*See Chapter 2.*)
If you are feeling shame, describe what about your bathroom makes you feel there is something wrong with you. (*See Chapter 3.*)	If you are dealing with perfectionism, how is that holding you back from taking care of your bathroom? (*See Chapter 3.*)
How are your values either shown or attacked in your bathroom? (*See Chapter 4.*)	What habits have led to the clutter in your bathroom? (*See Chapter 5.*)
What are your top five goals for your bathroom? (*See Chapter 6.*) **1.** **2.** **3.** **4.** **5.**	What steps will you take to reach those goals? (*See Chapter 6.*) **1.** **2.** **3.** **4.** **5.**

BATHROOM CHECKLIST

☐ Towels	☐ Cleaning Products	☐ Broken Trimmers	☐ Dusty Decor
☐ Skin Care	☐ Hairstyling Stuff	☐ Old Loofahs	☐ Shower Curtain
☐ Cosmetics	☐ Perfumes	☐ Bath Toys	☐ Makeup Bags
☐ Hair Products	☐ Body Lotions/Oils	☐ Hair Accessories	☐ Shaving Stuff
☐ OTC Medications	☐ Old Eyeglasses	☐ Empty Boxes	☐ First-Aid Supplies
☐ Prescriptions	☐ Hotel Toiletries	☐ Makeup Brushes	☐ Counter Clutter

After you have decluttered your bathroom, come back and answer these questions.

How do you feel when you think about your bathroom now?

What new habits will you be putting in place to maintain your bathroom?

Do you have any new goals for your bathroom since decluttering?

CHAPTER 10

HEY! WHOSE SHIT IS THIS?

When you declutter your home, you're wanting more control over the space you live in. If you live with other people, this becomes more complex.

More people means more variables. More hands touching things and using things. More chances that shit will get left out and start building to a crescendo of chaos.

This is when a decluttered home is most important. Clear organizational systems are a must.

Less crap in general means less possibility of that crap taking over.

Systems that everyone can understand and use easily make it more likely that they'll get used.

In our house, everything except my office is common space. We have two people who use all the same stuff. As I decluttered and organized, I had to keep that in mind. I had to be conscious of the fact that there were things I might think needed to go, but my husband wouldn't agree. There also had to be a clear reason why I moved something to a different place or organized it in a particular way.

The reality is that he hasn't known where many things are in our house for years.

He had gotten used to the chaos, and when I tidied up, he lost track of where things went.

He loves the change in the house, but he still doesn't know where to find paperclips or an extension cord.

☆ SUCCESS STRATEGY ☆

Labels, labels, and more labels.

I could try to change that by giving Shawn a tour of his own home, but it's easier to go get the thing myself or explain to him where it is in the moment.

Now, if we had kids, that wouldn't fly. I get away with a lot because it's only the two of us. The more people in a home, the clearer and more understandable it needs to be.

I don't know a single parent who wants to be explaining to people every day where to find things.

That's why I wrote this chapter, focused on families who have a hundred different needs and seem to always be going in different directions. Life gets chaotic enough. Having a house that can be quickly and easily put back together is a lifesaver.

THINGS THAT MAKE YOU GO HMMM . . .

LET'S FENG SHUI SOME SHIT!

I love me some Feng Shui. From the general philosophy for life to the energetic areas of your home to the colors and elements to use, I love it all. When we're talking about the common areas of your home, it's a great general space to start thinking Feng Shui.

DO	DON'T
Declutter! Make space for your life.	Try to Feng Shui the crap out of every little thing all at once. Take it slow and easy.
Consider all senses in decorating. Things like color, light, smells, sounds, textures.	Put things in your space just because they're "Feng Shui" if it isn't authentic to who you are.
One thing at a time. Less is more. Do one thing. Let it settle in, then do something else.	Underestimate the little things. Small changes can have a big impact.
Clean, fix, repair, or toss broken stuff first.	Have unused rooms. Like a formal dining room you never use. It creates all kinds of stagnant energy.
Pay attention to how everything works together. It all has energy, and you want it to work together.	Forget about the house as a whole. Don't just Feng Shui the bejesus out of one room and ignore the rest. Spread the love.
Set intentions. When you have the end result in mind, you're more likely to get there.	Forget about the outside! The energy of the outside of your home, even an apartment, affects the inside.
Listen to your gut. It knows you better than that Pinterest pin you've been ogling.	Assume it isn't working because your life didn't magically change. Feng Shui can take time to blend itself together in your space.
Consider the other people who live in the house. Everyone needs to feel comfortable, not just you.	Keep the curtains closed. Let the light in! Get sheers if you need privacy.
Be aware of your own impact on the energy of the home. Angry energy creates a sharp home. Curb the edges.	Get overwhelmed. Feng Shui comes with thousands of years of information. You won't figure it all out in a day.

WELL, SHIT, AM I READY FOR THIS?

The common areas of a home for the purposes of this chapter include, but sure as shit are not limited to:

- Living room
- Family room
- Entryway/mudroom
- Hallways
- Laundry room

It's a lot of space that everyone passes through. It can feel open and undefined—and very overwhelming.

It's understandable that these are not the spaces you want to think about. Kitchens and bedrooms and bathrooms all feel more contained.

When you're thinking about your readiness to deal with these spaces, be gentle with yourself. Yes, they may be the most visible, but this is sprawling space, which makes it tough to define. We tend to avoid the undefined.

- **Precontemplation:** "Everyone else just messes this place up. There's no reason to tidy it up just to have it torn back down."
- **Contemplation:** "Damn, I stepped on another Lego! Maybe tidy isn't such a bad idea."
- **Preparation:** "Oh, yeah, I'm getting this place under control, and everyone will have to deal with whatever new rules I come up with."

- **Action:** "Huh, there are like a hundred cat toys under the couch. And who put half a pizza puff under here? I'm glad I'm finally doing this. These people are disgusting!"
- **Maintenance:** "They're actually following the rules. How strange. So, all I had to do to get a tidy home was to clear it out, then be clear about how to live in it together? Fascinating."

What do you think?

- Is it a waste of time to focus on these areas at this point?
- Are you getting tired of the chaos, wishing there was a way it would all go away?
- Do you feel like you could pull yourself together to divide and conquer these areas?
- Are you in the middle of looking under couches and totally know what I'm talking about with the cat toys and lost food items?
- Have you faced it, lived it, and are working on keeping the family in line with the new systems?

Wherever you're at, be accepting of it. Try not to tell yourself you should be doing something else or something more. It will all come in time. Let's see if dealing with the emotional BS helps get you there.

SHITTY THINKING IN YOUR COMMON AREAS

Because this space is so visible, it comes with a lot of limiting beliefs and fears. This is the space everyone sees right away.

This is the space you'll feel some of the most judgment (real or imagined) in.

Limiting Beliefs: Not believing in your own ability to tame the chaos and stay on top of it is usually at the top of the list of limiting beliefs here.

You see the mayhem day to day, and you feel like no one listens to you when you tell them to pick up their crap. It feels like an uphill battle that you just do not want to wage every day.

You're going to have to take the risk to believe in yourself.

I also want you to understand that this is a part of the whole. Meaning, if this is the only space you tidy, it's unlikely to stay that way. Ick from other areas of the house will bleed over into the common areas.

However, when you tidy this space as part of an overarching plan to tidy the whole house, the new systems will seep in instead. It will become normal for everyone to put their crap away (possibly with a little bit of grumbling and periodic tantrums).

Like it or not, you are the model in this house. When you believe you can deal with this and you model it for everyone else, you'll be delighted with how they fall in line.

Fears: Fear can be a motivator. I don't like it as a motivator because it tends to be temporary and it's based on maintaining a heightened sense of pain. But if you're so afraid of looking like a slob, this might be the space you put most of your energy into. Then you hide the chaos behind closed doors.

> ☆ SUCCESS STRATEGY ☆
> **Never, and I do mean never, put something in the wrong place just to get rid of it.**

It's like wearing a mask. If people just see this space and you never let them see behind the metaphorical or literal curtain, you can pretend you've totally got your shit together. One of many issues with this approach is the fear you have that others will discover your dirty little secret and think less of you for it.

I'd far rather you keep this space clear and tidy out of the joy it brings you. This is using pleasure as your motivation.

Pleasure is the long-term motivator. When something feels good, you want more of it.

Maybe it's time to take the risk to have a home you feel good in. Maybe it's time to face those fears.

LETTING GO OF SOME SHIT

When you feel like you couldn't possibly keep up with a tidy home and you're perpetually afraid people are going to judge you for living in a sty, perfectionism and shame will be ever-present. You'll always feel like you're failing and will judge yourself before anyone else even gets a chance.

Perfectionism: You know that phenomenon where you see something so often that you stop seeing it at all? Like a note you put on your mirror to remind yourself to set your clothes out at night. It works for a while, then it becomes part of the mirror and your brain stops seeing it. This is what it's like when you first get a tattoo. You can't stop seeing it, then you forget it's there even when it's on your hand (I forget about the Om on my left hand *all* the time).

The same principle applies to clutter in common areas. You get so used to it being there that you kind of forget it's there, except for those moments when you feel drained by it all.

When you feel like nothing is good enough unless it's perfect, you might swing in the opposite direction of perfect to try to save yourself.

Ignore the piles. Ignore the tear in the couch. Ignore the stack of laundry that toppled onto the floor.

Your brain says, "I don't want to deal, so I'm going to pretend none of it's there."

You know that when you decide to actually deal with this mess, you're going to hate every second of it because you can't pretend it isn't there anymore.

This is how perfectionism screws you and keeps you stuck in an earlier Stage of Change.

Shame: When you hide things, it's usually a pretty good indicator that you're ashamed of something. So, how does that apply in spaces where you can't really hide anything because it's all out in the open?

That's the problem, it's all out in the open so you *can't* hide it. There are only so many closets and hidey-holes you can shove stuff into when friends come over. Common areas feel like the defining space of our homes. As soon as someone walks into your home, they're going to have a judgment, positive or negative.

This makes you judge yourself as being bad, faulty, and broken. When you feel like that, you have little to no motivation to do anything about it, because you figure you aren't worth the effort.

Stop judging yourself and give yourself a chance to feel proud of your entryway, proud of the living room where everyone sits to watch the game on Sunday.

Hiding isn't going to get you where you want to be.

THE SHIT YOU VALUE

Like I said, common areas feel like defining spaces in our homes. When people walk into your house, they get that all-important first impression people always talk about. Once you've dealt with your fear and shame, it's time to pick your head up and really define that space with your values.

First of all, I'm guessing a cluttered home doesn't fit with your values. That's part of why it feels so gross. You value things like cleanliness and clarity. In a cluttered home, those aren't represented.

Beyond those basics of why you like uncluttered spaces are the values you want to surround yourself with.

In the common areas of my house, you'll see pictures, posters, and other wall-hanging items telling you that we love:

- Travel to foreign lands.
- Music, mostly of the punk variety.
- Movies in genres of sci-fi, action-adventure.
- Warm, sunny beaches where no one wants anything from you.

We also value coziness, so you're going to see a lot of throw blankets and pillows on the couches. And, while I prefer a clean open space in my kitchen and bedroom, the cozy factor of the living spaces is increased with a "French salon" style of picture-hanging. That's a fancy way to say there's a lot of intentionally placed shit on the walls.

Common areas are where you spend most of your time. Let them reflect what you value. It will lift you up and encourage you in that authentic life thing we've talked about.

☆ SUCCESS STRATEGY ☆

Not sure how to represent your values in your common areas? Hit up Pinterest. You can see what other people have done with their homes and respond with "Oo! Yes, that's totally us!" or "OMG, why would anyone ever do that?"

GETTING OVER YOUR SHITTY HABITS

Systems are vital to the running of a household. This is most obvious in the common areas of your house. Shitty habits are the downfall of systems.

- ✕ Kids leaving their backpacks on the floor of the mudroom.
- ✕ Toys not getting put away until you step on a Lego and threaten to throw it all out.
- ✕ Letting books and magazines pile up on end tables.
- ✕ Eating in the living room and leaving dishes out.
- ✕ Dumping the clean laundry on a chair or sofa, swearing you'll get to it later.
- ✕ Shoes and coats getting dropped wherever and never getting put away.

You know, stuff like that.

When there's a lot going on, it's easy to let shit go "for now." But for now becomes forever when it's all so overwhelming you can't deal.

This is your domain. Decide on some systems to keep things put away and decluttered. Agree on them with your spouse. Sit the kids down and tell them what's what. You may have to help out littles for a bit until they get it, but they can catch on really quickly so long as it's modeled for them to keep on going.

Get those systems in place, and clutter will be a thing of the past!

☆ SUCCESS STRATEGY ☆

Have baskets or bins labeled for everyone in the house. Once a day, clear stuff off flat surfaces and off the ground, then drop them in the basket of whoever they belong to. At least once a week, have everyone empty their basket and put crap away.

LET'S SET THE SHIT OUT OF SOME GOALS

The common areas can encompass a huge part of your home. Goal-setting will be critical to keeping on task, and motivated.

- **Small Victory:** Clear crap off the end tables.
- **Big Impact:** Gather up all the shoes and coats to declutter and organize.
- **Irritant:** Scrub the water rings off the glass coffee table.
- **Worst:** Pull the couches out to clear out and vacuum under.

Setting goals for the areas of your house that everyone uses takes thought and planning. My advice is to take it one room at a time. If you hop from room to room dealing with one pile after the other, you end up with a lot of unfinished projects. Focusing on one room until it's done gives you a lot more bang for your buck and creates motivation to head into the next room.

☆ SUCCESS STRATEGY ☆

Use essential oil aromatherapy in common areas for mood and healing, like my favorite for Shawn's vestibular migraines of lemon eucalyptus, wintergreen, and lavender.

THE TAKEAWAY

The common areas of your house come with big impact and are what you and your guests see first when you come into the house. Letting go of any shame over the state of your home and taking action will give you a sense of being in control of your home again.

It got this way because there were no systems in place. Get it decluttered and set those systems up so you never have to go through this again.

MAKING IT REAL

Now that you've worked on yourself, and you've reviewed the process of decluttering your common areas, it's time to check in, get honest, and create a plan.

Before you declutter your common areas, answer these questions.

What do you feel when you think about decluttering your common areas? Check all that apply: ☐ **Angry** ☐ **Hopeless** ☐ **Anxious** ☐ **Joyful** ☐ **Ashamed** ☐ **Loving** ☐ **Doubtful** ☐ **Overwhelmed** ☐ **Excited** ☐ **Sad** ☐ **Hopeful** ☐ **Other** ________	How would you like to feel about your common areas? Please describe:
What Stage of Change do you see yourself in when you think about your common areas? (*See Chapter 1.*) Why?	If you haven't reached Action, what do you think you need to do to move into the next stage? (*See Chapter 1.*)
What limiting beliefs have kept you from decluttering your common areas? (*See Chapter 2.*)	What fears do you have about beginning to declutter your common areas? (*See Chapter 2.*)
If you are feeling shame, describe what about your common areas makes you feel there is something wrong with you. (*See Chapter 3.*)	If you are dealing with perfectionism, how is that holding you back from taking care of your common areas? (*See Chapter 3.*)
How are your values either shown or attacked in your common areas? (*See Chapter 4.*)	What habits have led to the clutter in your common areas? (*See Chapter 5.*)
What are your top five goals for your common areas? (*See Chapter 6.*) **1.** **2.** **3.** **4.** **5.**	What steps will you take to reach those goals? (*See Chapter 6.*) **1.** **2.** **3.** **4.** **5.**

COMMON AREAS CHECKLIST

☐ Toys	☐ Seasonal Items	☐ Decor	☐ Cords
☐ Step Stools	☐ Sporting Items	☐ Broken Items	☐ Candles
☐ End Tables	☐ Sunglasses	☐ Rugs	☐ Video Games
☐ School Supplies	☐ Reading Glasses	☐ Throw Pillows	☐ Musical Stuff
☐ Shoes	☐ Pet Toys	☐ Throw Blankets	☐ Liquor Cabinet
☐ Books	☐ Knickknacks	☐ Technology	☐ Bags

After you have decluttered your common areas, come back and answer these questions.

How do you feel when you think about your common areas now?

What new habits will you be putting in place to maintain your common areas?

Do you have any new goals for your common areas since decluttering?

CHAPTER 11

NO MORE SHITTY SLEEP

My bedroom is a sanctuary. It is used only for the things it is intended for. It is where I curl up when I'm sick. It's where I spend lazy Sunday mornings with my husband. It's the calmest room in my house. It has purpose.

Before my decluttering, I could not have said that. My bedroom was a wreck! Many, *many* bags of donations later, I had my truly clutter-free bedroom.

My energy was no longer being sucked out of me by the chaos hidden in drawers and behind doors.

I even changed the contents of the drawers under my bed to be only soft things that gave off no sharp vibes that interrupt sleep.

Once I had the room under control, I ached to get it repainted. The forest green that had seemed so perfect in 2005 was no longer doing it for me. I wanted my life light and airy!

The bedroom got painted a pale sky blue, which inspired the color scheme of the comforter set (complete with far more decorative pillows than anyone needs) and the wall hangings. The wall over my dresser that had sported two nails and nothing else since I had moved the mirror from there years before now has an intentional art piece that ties the whole room together.

Every morning, I make my bed now. Before decluttering, I had said I just wasn't a make-the-bed kind of person. Remember, I had labeled myself a slob and a pig. Slobs and pigs don't make their beds. They say things like "Leaving it unmade allows the sheets to air out." I'm totally serious. This is what I would tell people.

☆ SUCCESS STRATEGY ☆

Make your damn bed every morning. It might not give you a sense of joy at the time, but walking into that room later in the day, it will make all the difference in how you feel.

As I said, now I make my bed every morning. Even on the days that Shawn sleeps in and I forget to make it until four in the afternoon, it still gets made so I go to bed that night in serenity instead of chaos. When I've pulled the comforter up, turned the top of it down, sprayed everything with my homemade linen spray, and settled all of the decorative pillows in place, the room is complete and I take a nice deep sigh of satisfaction. This is a room that invites sweet dreams.

Okay, I just reread that last bit, and it sounded so corny I almost fucking choked. But it's all true. I swear! That being said, Shawn would like me to tell you that the bed-making thing is against his better judgment, as he would still prefer to get into a rumpled mess of a bed that wraps around him like a big cuddly snake. To each their own. He can do that when I'm out of town.

In the meantime, he knows he needs to be nice to me or else I won't set up his aromatherapy (lavender, bergamot, and frankincense) or the battery-operated candles that give the soft glow he likes to drift off to sleepyland with.

☆ SUCCESS STRATEGY ☆

Make a homemade linen spray in an 8 oz glass spray bottle with 60 drops of lavender, 30 drops of bergamot, 30 drops of frankincense, and 3 tablespoons of witch hazel. Fill with distilled water and spray your sheets every morning when you make the bed.

WELL, SHIT, AM I READY FOR THIS?

You can close the door to your room or the kids' rooms and pretend they aren't there, making it easy to put off decluttering bedrooms. But then you're tripping over stuff, there are baskets of laundry being picked through on the floor, and you're perpetually telling your children to clean up their rooms. (Okay, that last one is going to happen no matter what, sorry.)

- **Precontemplation:** "It's just a bedroom; all I do is sleep in it. Why would I need to clean it?"
- **Contemplation:** "Ugh, okay, maybe my sleep would be better if I wasn't surrounded by all of this crap. Heck, maybe my sex life would be better too."

- **Preparation:** "Okay, clearly this has to change. This is not a restful or healing room in any way, shape, or form."
- **Action:** "Oh, wow, the bed looks so inviting made up with the new comforter, and it's awesome not tripping on anything getting into bed!"
- **Maintenance:** "New rules: make the bed, put the laundry away, and never leave something in here that doesn't belong here. Man, I never want to leave this room!"

When you decide you are a priority, you'll be ready to deal with your own bedroom.

When you decide it's more of a priority to help your kids declutter their rooms than the other hundred things you need to do, you'll get them going. You will not regret spending time on these rooms.

Having a bedroom that you can walk into and feel relieved by, instead of stressed, will change your sleep. You'll have a greater chance of waking up feeling prepared for the day.

SHITTY THINKING IN YOUR BEDROOM

Bedrooms are highly personal; that's where the limiting beliefs and fears come in. We're going to talk about clothing and closets on their own in the next chapter, so for now, we're just talking about the room itself.

Limiting Beliefs: Depending on whether you're talking about your bedroom or your kids', your limiting beliefs may vary.

- **Kids' room:** "He's just going to mess it up again, why help him tidy it up?" Or "She's so particular and is probably going to scream at me, which I just can't handle, so I'm not even going to suggest we declutter her room."

- ✕ **Yours:** "Stuff from other areas of the house just always ends up in here, so there's no point in trying to change it." Or "I've never had a tidy room. There's no way I'll be able to keep it tidy now."

Fears: Your fears of getting in over your head or starting something that will take forever to complete can get in the way of decluttering bedrooms.

Because bedrooms are contained spaces, it can feel like you must finish what you started without interruption. The reality is that life comes with interruptions.

Create solutions to your fears.

Heck, your fears of what you'll find in helping your teenage son declutter his room could be very realistic, but the solution isn't to ignore the problem.

We deal with fears by facing them head-on. Even teenage boys.

LETTING GO OF SOME SHIT

Maybe you have a specific picture of what you want your bedroom to look like. Perhaps quiet and serene. Maybe sexy and sultry. Whatever it is, waiting for all of the pieces to come together before you take action may mean you're sleeping in a half-done bedroom for years. The next thing you know, you're closing that door any time anyone comes over because you're ashamed of the state of affairs.

☆ SUCCESS STRATEGY ☆

Don't bother creating design and decorating plans for a cluttered bedroom. When it's decluttered, you can create all the plans you want, and you'll be more likely to follow through right away because of how excited you are.

I recently brought a friend up to my room, even though I knew I hadn't had a chance to make the bed, because I wanted to show her my closet and dresser drawers with all of their file folded clothing (*see Chapter 12*). Did I love that it wasn't in perfect styled shape? Nope. Did I really care? Nope. That's the fun of letting shit go.

Perfectionism: "I'm not going to put the new comforter on until we've had a chance to paint the walls. I want to have it all just right before I break that out." In the meantime, years pass with the comforter sitting on the floor of your bedroom with walls the same color they've always been and that ratty old comforter still on the bed.

That's a true story. I was terribly dismayed when I was at a client's house and heard this story. Three years had passed, and she still hadn't used the comforter that she thought was so beautiful.

The funny thing is that when she capitulated and put the comforter on her bed, she was mysteriously suddenly ready to hire painters. Hmm, I wonder why?

She'd been holding herself back from something pleasurable, waiting for the exact right conditions to use it. Having something she loved on her bed made the walls look so awful she simply had to do something about it.

Shame: It's too easy to ignore your bedroom and put up with less than what you deserve. Then you're left with a space that you don't want anyone else to see because you feel ashamed of its state.

Imagine what that does to your sleep, to be in a room you don't even like.

I'm not saying a room you feel proud of will cure your sleep apnea; I'm saying the energy of a tidy, calm, loved room will positively impact your whole sleep experience. And you need your sleep!

THINGS THAT MAKE YOU GO HMMM . . .

This is a book about decluttering. It brings images of wide-open, uncluttered spaces to mind. But what if you have a tiny house? What if you have a tiny bedroom? What to do? This is when the ideal meets the real. Having a lot of stuff in a room does not mean it's cluttered. It would be lovely if we could all have spacious bedrooms with lots of closet space. Tell that to my college efficiency that stuffed a living space, bedroom, kitchen, closet, and bathroom all into the space my current bedroom (which is not big) has.

Sometimes you need a few ingenious ideas to create the systems that will keep a small space uncluttered.

Under-the-bed shoe drawers.

Feng Shui asks that if you must put things under your bed, that they be soft. Well, we're trying, okay?

Under-the-bed drawers for everything else.

Here's where your truly soft things like sweaters, blankets, and Halloween costumes (or is that just my house?) go.

Labeled drawers in the closet for underthings.

As much as I love my folded underwear and socks, it isn't necessary. You can toss them in bins in that space under your shirts in the closet. With labels!!

Shelves around the top of your walls.

I don't know about you, but I'm not using the top foot of space on my walls. You could keep nicely organized stuff up there.

Use the corners!

So much lost space. But there are tons of organizing units you can find that are designed to fit into a corner.

Wall-mounted jewelry.

There's always some chunk of wall that's too narrow for other stuff. That wall has necklaces on it in my closet.

Over-the-door shoe caddy for anything.

Sure, you could put shoes in it, but you can also put stuffed animals, mittens, socks, purses, etc. in there.

Over-the-door baseball cap organizer.

This is what I came up with for the 30+ caps my husband owns and wears!

Wall hooks galore.

Again, there's wall space that doesn't always get used well. Bags, sporting equipment, instruments, and so forth.

Add a rod to your closet.

If you only have the one rod and there's unused space under the short things, add another line and let your clothes breathe.

A standing clothes rack.

The room I sublet for a summer in college was originally the parlor, so no closets. Wardrobe racks with mobile shelves were a perfect fit.

Dollar store bins.

I always say you don't have to spend a lot of money to be organized. Hit up a dollar store or two and find your own creative solutions.

Wall hamper.

You don't want your dirty clothes on the ground, and if you don't have room for a hamper you can find a solution.

Rolling carts.

These can serve multiple purposes and be in more than one place, depending on the need.

Storage ottoman.

If you like to have a place to sit in your bedroom, ottomans are nice. They're even nicer if they double as extra storage.

THE SHIT YOU VALUE

Let's talk about the things that happen in bedrooms. There's the obvious, like sleep and sex. Then there's getting dressed, healing when you're sick or injured, getting quiet time with a book, snuggling with loved ones, crying when you're sad or overwhelmed, laughing when one of those loved ones does something silly—the list goes on.

These are all things that represent values of things like safety, security, health, family, preparedness, laughter, and comfort. These are all things that lend themselves to the gentle energy the room you sleep in needs.

There are other things people do in bed, like work, pay bills, scroll on their phones, and argue, that do not lend themselves to that energy. These things suggest that achievement, money, technology, and power are higher values.

I'm not saying one or the other is what you should be doing or not doing. In all transparency, I'm writing this while sitting on my (made) bed with my cat. I'm here because I needed a change of scenery, but also because I feel comfortable in my bedroom and I'm not much of a sit-at-a-desk kind of gal.

This is an exception, though, not a rule. I do not keep work stuff in here. My phone and my computer live and get charged in my office. The bedroom is a sacred room.

What I value dictates that I can use the energy in this room to help me do work now and then, but this room is designed for bedroom stuff, not general life stuff.

Your job for your bedroom is to figure out what values you want to prioritize in that space. Decide how that helps you.

If it's possible to keep more energetic things like work and arguments out of the space, all the better for the purpose of peaceful sleep. But no one gets to tell you how your values are represented in any area of your home, especially not somewhere as precious as your bedroom.

GETTING OVER YOUR SHITTY HABITS

I just talked about how your behaviors in your bedroom reflect your values. Your habits are your behaviors. These things are all intertwined. As you read this section, think about how that connection shows up in your own bedroom.

You dash into your room to get dressed. You collapse in here at the end of a busy day. You hide in here when you're sick and too tired to do anything else. You get out of bed bleary-eyed in the morning when you don't have the time or inclination to think about clutter.

We have two forms of shitty habits in here:

- The shit you do in bed that's totally interruptive of your sleep.
- The things you do that allow clutter to build up on every flat surface, including the floor.

SHITTY THINGS YOU DO IN BED

If you say your bed is for sleeping and sex, there are a lot of things that don't have anything to do with either of those that I know you're doing. Look, I don't expect you to follow what I'm saying to the letter. I absolutely do all of the things I'm about to talk about, but I know it isn't a good idea. When I find myself getting too deep in the habit of doing these things, I hit my reset button with a few rules.

Having arguments in bed: I know you know how awful it is to go to bed angry. Unfortunately, not all arguments are solved because it's bedtime. And it's tough to find a place to argue other than your room if kids are home. The ultimate solution is to not bother with arguing. But if you are going to, take it outside, in the basement, to a park, honestly—I don't care where. Just leave shitty energy out of your bedroom.

Scrolling through social media: I talk to a lot of people who really enjoy a little social media scroll before bed. I don't want to take that away from you if it isn't a problem. But if you find you lose an hour or two and are habitually not getting enough sleep because you went down the rabbit hole, it may be time to take a break.

Watching TV: I want to be very honest and tell you that I have a TV in my bedroom, and I do watch it now that we get streaming up there. That being said, this is a "do as I say, not as I do" situation.

There isn't anything evil about TV; it's just that the flickering images can interrupt your sleep. If you're sleeping fine, cool, rock on with your Hulu.

But if you're having any sleeping issues, try not falling asleep to the TV and read instead.

Eating: The bed is simply not for eating. How many times do you have to tell your kids to stop taking food to their rooms? You don't want bugs and mice in their rooms, so I hope you don't want them in your room either!

Writing to-do lists: Sometimes writing a few of your to-do's down on a pad of paper next to the bed can help get them out of your head so you can fall asleep. But if you habitually write tomorrow's to-do list in bed, you're revving your brain up to think about everything you have to do, which is not conducive to sleep. Write your list before getting in bed. Easy solution, right?

CLUTTERING UP FLAT SURFACES

Using your room as a catchall: Throwing things into your room because you don't know where else to put them is one of the shittiest habits in a cluttered home. Everything needs to have a home. Take the sixty seconds and put the thing away instead.

Dressers: When you walk into your bedroom holding something small, it's easy to set it down on your dresser and then walk away, forgetting about it. One thing clients tell me they do all the time is pull the tag off new clothes, then set the tag on the dresser instead of throwing it away.

☆ SUCCESS STRATEGY ☆

Take everything off your dresser and set it on your bed. Take each of those things to their home. You can't get in bed tonight until that stuff is all gone, and if it just gets put back on the dresser, that's cheating.

Bedside tables: The stuff next to your head when you sleep does affect you. Piles of books you keep meaning to read remind you of your unfinished tasks. Empty water bottles and other trash clutter your dreams. Thermometers and medications from that time you had the flu keep you stuck in an ill frame of mind. Clear it out and get some sleep!

Floors: Yes, floors are a flat surface. (At least I really hope floors are a flat surface in your home; otherwise, there's a serious problem.) Floors are meant for furniture and feet. Stop setting the laundry basket down on the floor and walking past it over and over before doing something with it. Stop dropping things in a corner of your room for lack of a better place to put them. Find a better place!

LET'S SET THE SHIT OUT OF SOME GOALS!

Now that you're jazzed to have a tidy oasis as your bedroom instead of a hellhole of chaos, it's time to set your goals. What do you want to start with?

- **Small Victory:** How about clearing all of the trash from your bedside table?
- **Big Impact:** Maybe it would feel really good to clear off the clothes that are covering the chair you put in this room so you could curl up with a good book (like this one, wink, wink).
- **Irritant:** Ugh, what about something like that pile of mail that somehow ended up on your dresser and you keep forgetting to take downstairs to go through?
- **Worst:** Or it could be time to go through that pile of... well, everything that has grown and taken over the floor of your bedroom.

Be honest with yourself as to what you are ready to tackle. Being clear about your goals will make it easier to follow through in this room that no one else sees and therefore is easy to leave to the last.

I also talked about shitty habits that have nothing to do with physical clutter. You will need to see what affects what. Is it difficult for you to set goals to change the habit of eating in bed while the bedroom is still a mess? Or is it easier to start tidying the room when you've committed to not eating in bed anymore?

THE TAKEAWAY

Your bedroom needs to be sacred. Your sleep needs to be sacred. This very personal and intimate space needs to be sacred.

Stop putting it off to the last.

I was someone who didn't pay a ton of attention to my bedroom. I didn't make my bed, I tossed clothes on the floor, and I stacked shit up on all of my flat surfaces. Then I cleared it out, got a beautiful comforter, painted, and hung a couple of super-intentional things on the walls (very minimal). Voilà! I had a room that I wanted to make the bed in because when I did, it changed the room into one that I loved stepping into.

I'm going to deal with your clothes in the next chapter, but it's hard to deal with your clothes when your room is a mess. You'll have to make a bit of a mess when you go through your clothing, so you don't want to have that mess joining with a preexisting mess to create a Godzilla-sized mess. That's overwhelming.

Get your room under control. Then it's time to enter the closet.

MAKING IT REAL

Now that you've worked on yourself, and you've reviewed the process of decluttering your bedroom, it's time to check in, get honest, and create a plan.

Before you declutter your bedroom, answer these questions.

What do you feel when you think about decluttering your bedroom? Check all that apply: ☐ **Angry** ☐ **Hopeless** ☐ **Anxious** ☐ **Joyful** ☐ **Ashamed** ☐ **Loving** ☐ **Doubtful** ☐ **Overwhelmed** ☐ **Excited** ☐ **Sad** ☐ **Hopeful** ☐ **Other** ________	How would you like to feel about your bedroom? Please describe:
What Stage of Change do you see yourself in when you think about your bedroom? (*See Chapter 1.*) Why?	If you haven't reached Action, what do you think you need to do to move into the next stage? (*See Chapter 1.*)
What limiting beliefs have kept you from decluttering your bedroom? (*See Chapter 2.*)	What fears do you have about beginning to declutter your bedroom? (*See Chapter 2.*)
If you are feeling shame, describe what about your bedroom makes you feel there is something wrong with you. (*See Chapter 3.*)	If you are dealing with perfectionism, how is that holding you back from taking care of your bedroom? (*See Chapter 3.*)
How are your values either shown or attacked in your bedroom? (*See Chapter 4.*)	What habits have led to the clutter in your bedroom? (*See Chapter 5.*)
What are your top five goals for your bedroom? (*See Chapter 6.*) **1.** **2.** **3.** **4.** **5.**	What steps will you take to reach those goals? (*See Chapter 6.*) **1.** **2.** **3.** **4.** **5.**

BEDROOM CHECKLIST

☐ Sheet Sets	☐ Furniture	☐ Luggage	☐ Stuffed Animals
☐ Extra Blankets	☐ Broken Items	☐ Purses	☐ Slippers
☐ Comforters	☐ Lamps	☐ Old Hampers	☐ CPAP Equipment
☐ Pillows	☐ Books	☐ Cosmetics	☐ Essential Oils
☐ Knickknacks	☐ Mattress Pads	☐ Vanity Items	☐ Sleep Masks
☐ Decor	☐ Extra Blankets	☐ Candles	☐ Sexual Aids

After you have decluttered your bedroom, come back and answer these questions.

How do you feel when you think about your bedroom now?

What new habits will you be putting in place to maintain your bedroom?

Do you have any new goals for your bedroom since decluttering?

CHAPTER 12

WELL, SHIT, HALF MY CLOTHES STILL HAVE TAGS

When you say the magic word *declutter*, most people immediately think of closets full to bursting with clothing. All that clothing can get really overwhelming really quickly.

Before I get too deep into this, I want to just say this: Gentlemen! Do not skip over this chapter because you think too much clothing is a "girly" issue. I see you. I see all your baseball caps, your excessive number of sneakers, your overflowing closet of suits in various sizes. I see all your hoodies and your golf shirts and your hockey jerseys. This is an intervention.

Okay. As you were.

One popular method of decluttering clothing is to start by pulling all of your clothes together into one great big pile. I mean *all* of your clothes. From every closet, out of the laundry, out of the car, gym bags, mudrooms, or wherever clothing is hiding in your house.

As overwhelming as this method sounds, I actually like it. It gets the job done at one time, so that little pockets of clothing don't get missed. Unfortunately, I don't think it's terribly realistic. It certainly isn't how I decluttered my clothing.

- ✕ I didn't have two days to focus on my clothes.
- ✕ I needed to keep living in and using my bedroom.
- ✕ I have a small house. I don't have an extra space where I could put all of those clothes while I went through them.
- ✕ I might have been vulnerable to giving up and letting this project go on for weeks because of how daunting it was.

Instead, I took it drawer by drawer, then moved to the closet, where I did it category by category.

I think it's important to let your gut guide you in this. Yes, trusting yourself is in fact a big part of decluttering your home. This whole listen-to-your-gut thing is important. Otherwise, you're trying to create change in your world by someone else's rules.

For me, starting with the dresser drawers made the most sense because they were small, controlled spaces. It started one Friday morning when I was lying in bed watching decluttering and cleaning videos on YouTube. I was addicted to those like porn for a long time. My eye kept going to the drawer that held my tank tops.

This drawer was the bane of my existence. How do you organize tank tops so that you know where they are and what you have? I had tried over and over, having settled on a quadrant system, where four different styles of tank were layered in each quadrant.

1. Band tanks
2. Sports-related tanks
3. Workout tanks
4. Fancy tanks

It wasn't a terrible system as systems go. It was intentional, and there was method to my madness; but no matter what, there were still tops I never wore because I never saw them.

One of the YouTube videos I had watched that morning was a How to Get Your Shit Together (www.howtogyst.com) tutorial on Marie Kondo's file folding. This was before I had read Ms. Kondo's books, yet I had heard about this method of folding clothes and thought it was fascinating. But I thought there was no way I'd ever be able to keep my stuff that way.

Limiting belief, anyone?

Bullshit. I can do anything I want to do. And I wanted to do this. I've seen videos by other people in which they have said the same thing, that they wouldn't be able to keep up with it. I say, how the hell do you know until you try?

**File folding isn't for everyone.
I ask you to give it a try, though.**

I have a number of clients who have tried this method and love it. I have others for whom we've adopted a cube drawer system where the category of clothing for that cube is tossed in unceremoniously to be dug through later. This method gives me hives to think about, but it really works for some people, especially those with ADHD.

**Don't ever think that what works for you is
wrong because it's different from someone
else's method. If it works, it works.**

But back to my poor tank tops.

I figured one little drawer couldn't take that long, so why not give it a go? Look, generally speaking I want you to have a plan, to set goals, and to follow through with them. However, if you have a moment when you feel inspired, even driven, to do something, go for it. I only ask that you be realistic about the time it will take versus the time you have so that you aren't leaving unfinished projects all over the house.

I took everything out and piled it all on my bed. You *must* empty the drawer. If you leave something in there for any reason, you can't be totally sure you've completely decluttered.

Then I picked up one after the other and asked myself:

- Do I wear this?
- Do I love this?

The problem I had before was that I kept organizing shit I didn't wear and didn't really love. At least I've never been prone to keeping things that are stained or have holes in them, so that wasn't an issue.

The bottom half of each of those four stacks held crap I never wore. So out it went!

The remainder got file folded within an inch of its life and tucked back into the drawer. In the end, I had a drawer:

- Where I could see everything I had.
- That was only three quarters full.

I was amazed by the space I had left, and mildly giddy over the tidiness of the little rows of bundled tank tops. This led to going through my T-shirt drawer next. A hefty decluttering of T-shirts later, and I had combined two drawers. WTF!?

One by one (literally often one per day), I decluttered, moved, and folded everything in my drawers, including my underwear. That's right. Even my underwear is folded into little packages that stand up so I can see what I have.

No more holes in the lace of my undies. Is it just me, or do your thumbs go straight through that flimsy fabric too? No more waiting to do the laundry for forty-five days because that's how much underwear I had. I have as much as fits in the single row I created for them.

☆ SUCCESS STRATEGY ☆

Use drawer dividers to create controlled space in your drawers.

The closet was next. Shawn and I share a very small walk-in closet. It's a square. One wall is all shoes, both of ours. One wall is the random crap that you put in a closet, plus a couple of shelves of his clothing. The third wall is hanging clothes: a four-foot rod with my clothes on the bottom and a four-foot rod for him on top. There is another foot for dresses and a few Halloween costumes.

I had this closet custom-made when the original crappy white wire shelf that held all of my hanging clothes gave out and crashed to the ground the night before we left on vacation for two weeks. Thanks for that. I had totally forgotten about it until we got home and I went into the closet. Fuck!

☆ SUCCESS STRATEGY ☆

Basic closets waste space. Spend a little cash for some sort of custom closet organization. Get it from somewhere like Target and install it yourself or hire a professional to design it.

For my clothes, I did them in two chunks:

- Shoes
- Clothing

I did the shoes first. I had "decluttered" them many times before, and yet there were still shoes piled on top of shoes on my nice, tidy shoe shelves. I kind of doubted the necessity of taking *all* of them out at once, until I actually did it.

I got them all on the floor of my bedroom and lined them up like a little shoe firing squad. It was so much easier to look at them and realize which ones I really didn't wear or even like.

If your shoes are dusty, you don't wear them. It's time to pull out a bugle to play Taps and say good-bye.

One by one, the shoes I loved were put in the "keep" pile. Then the ones I liked or needed, like water shoes. Not the prettiest things in the world, but damn do I need them when I'm tubing down a Midwestern river with a rocky bottom.

In the end, I cut about a third of my shoes. I put the remainder back but still had to maneuver them to fit on the shelves. I have since pared them down to only what actually fits in the space. Now, if I get a new pair, one has to go; otherwise, they won't fit.

SUCCESS STRATEGY

The One-In-One-Out Rule: When you buy something new, something else has to go. Stick to this, and your wardrobe will never get out of control again.

The hanging clothes were the same. Everybody out of the pool! Piled up on my bed, it looked like a monumental task. But taking it one piece at a time and not focusing on the pile itself helped it to not be overwhelming.

- Do I love this?
- Do I wear this?
- How do I feel when I wear this?

That last one helped with the pieces I wasn't totally sure of. I had to put a lot of things on to remind myself of how I felt in them. It takes some time to get in tune with how you feel in clothes. Not "How much did I pay for this?" or "Is this something I think I'm supposed to like?" But "Do I feel good in it?"

I've had my clothes divided into short sleeves and long sleeves, then by color, and on all-matching black plastic tube hangers since 2002, when we still lived in our first apartment together. So I put all of the *love*s and *yes, I do wear*s back into the closet in order.

Since then, I've gotten all matching white wooden hangers. They take up more room, which means I have less space to play with. It's a good way to keep your closet in line. Like the shoes, when I run out of hangers because I've bought something new, I have to get rid of something else.

I've had clients try to cheat the system by getting those skinny flocked hangers so that they can shove as much as humanly possible into their closets. My issue with that is that you're starting out with a goal of overstuffing your closet, which is the opposite of this decluttering thing we're talking about. Plus clothes that are stuffed together have no ability to breathe. Yes, cloth needs to breathe. Unless you enjoy wearing clothes that smell slightly unfresh or even musty and funky. But, hey, you do you, boo.

☆ SUCCESS STRATEGY ☆

Make the stuff fit the container. Don't try to make the container fit the stuff. If you have X amount of room, work with that. Don't pretend you can bend physics.

It's now habit for me to look at my clothing with a critical eye and ask myself if I really like or love things or if I'm keeping them for some other, less logical reason. If all else fails, I give the item in question one last try by wearing it for a day. I once ripped a sweater off in the middle of my work day because I realized I hated it. I had to spend the rest of the day working in the only mildly stained tank top I had under it.

In the end, I have found I always have something to wear because I only own things I like. It's been years and years since the last time I stood in the middle of my closet with a sea of discarded clothing at my feet, screaming about how I had nothing to wear, while my terrified hubby looked on, trying to stay as still as possible so I wouldn't turn on him.

WELL, SHIT, AM I READY FOR THIS?

I've had plenty of clients who wanted to tackle their clothes but simply were not ready for it because it looked like such a daunting task. This wardrobe intimidation can exist for a lot of reasons.

- You have multiple closets with clothes in them and pulling it all together sounds horrible.
- You have totes of clothes that once fit you and you feel like you shouldn't get rid of that stuff "just in case."

- Facing the various sizes in your closet may trigger your frustration with your current body.
- There are so many piles, baskets, additional drawer units, and everything else under the sun jammed in your closet that you have no idea where to start.

Your readiness will coincide with your willingness to face the dragon hiding in your closet. One young woman wanted my help with the clothes that had literally taken over four rooms in her home, spilling out of half-opened drawers, stacked in totes, hanging on multiple standing racks. But she simply was not ready. She was in Contemplation and wanted to be in Action, but other things in her life that needed to be taken care of for her to get there were too big for her to face at the time she reached out to me.

☆ SUCCESS STRATEGY ☆

Don't give up on yourself just because you're not where you wish you were. Be gentle and patient. You can get there.

- **Precontemplation:** "It doesn't matter if I declutter this closet or not. I'll just buy more clothes, and it'll be a mess in a week anyway."
- **Contemplation:** "It might actually be nice to be able to find something in here without having to use both arms to shove stuff aside."
- **Preparation:** "That's it—this has to change. The sweaters on the shelf are rising up into the hanging clothes. There's going to be an avalanche if I don't do something radical quickly."
- **Action:** "Holy heck, seriously, I don't even remember

buying half this stuff. It's like shopping in my own wardrobe!"

× **Maintenance:** "One in, one out. As long as I'm sticking to that rule, this will never get out of hand again."

Remember Colleen, who had tackled the bottomless pit under her bathroom sink? She had nothing in her dresser drawers except stuff she never used, because everything she did use was in baskets on the floor. It started out as not having enough time to put things away, then it turned into years of preparing to declutter so she didn't think it made sense to put things away that she was going to pull out again anyway. She ended up so lost in her own room that she had no idea where to start. I stood in her room with her and pointed at a basket, saying "Start with that one."

She was ready for Action; she just needed a little help. Think about that. If you feel you're ready but could use some help, bring in your best friend, your sister, or anyone you trust—not to make choices for you, but to keep you on track.

I want you to know how fucking proud I was of her the day she truly took control of her bedroom and stopped putting everyone in her life ahead of herself. It was a couple of years after that day that I stood in her room with her. She had moved in and out of the Stages of Change, and then one day she had planted her feet so firmly in Action that nothing could move her.

It took three weeks (and the periodic support of her twin sister) to work through the baskets, the dresser, and two closets, but she did it. She even had her husband paint the closets. She released so much crap that no longer served her that she moved herself into the smaller of the closets and gave the larger one to her husband.

Colleen used every single mental and physical skill in this book and stormed her own castle.

THINGS THAT MAKE YOU GO HMMM . . .

FILE FOLDING

File folding is a method of folding clothes popularized by the organizing expert and author Marie Kondo. You fold your clothes into little squares or rectangles so that they can stand up and fill your drawers as if you were filling a filing cabinet.

Why do I love it?
It takes up less room.
You can see what you have.
It makes getting dressed easier.
You can tell what clothes you never wear.

I'm giving you a quick breakdown as to how to fold a few key items here. For additional instruction, my favorite video is on the YouTube page *How to Get Your Shit Together*, March 24, 2016, *KonMari Folding: How To Fold Clothes Using The KonMari Method.*

Shirts

1. Lay the shirt out flat, with the front side or the most recognizable side (e.g., the design on a T-shirt) facing down.
2. Fold one side of the shirt across the center.
3. Fold the sleeve of the shirt back.
4. Fold the other side of the shirt across the center, stopping a little before the edge.
5. Fold the other sleeve back.
6. Fold the top of the shirt toward the bottom of the shirt, stopping a little before the edge.
7. Fold the folded edge of the shirt over toward the bottom.
8. Fold over the shirt once more to create a small rectangle.

Pants/Jeans

1. Fold the pants in half widthwise, with the pant legs stacked.
2. If the seat sticks out, fold it over against the legs of the pants.
3. Fold the ankles of the pants up toward the waist, leaving a gap before the waistband.
4. Fold the folded edge of the pants over toward the waistband up one third.
5. Fold over the pants once more to create a small rectangle.

Underwear

1. Start by laying the underwear out flat, with the back side facing up.
2. Fold the bottom of the underwear up toward the waistband.
3. Fold one side over to the center.
4. Fold the other side over.
5. Roll the bottom of the underwear up toward the waistband.
6. Turn over so that the waistband is at the front.

Don't get overwhelmed by these descriptions. I've kept my drawers like this since 2018 with no issue. What I allowed for was developing my own way to get to the desired outcome. As in, I don't tuck the little bit of the seat of pants in to create a "perfect" square. It's imperfect. I'm okay with that. I also fold my underwear totally differently than these instructions, because it works for me.

Always take the initial instructions as suggestions and then allow for doing it exactly that way or developing your own way.

SHITTY THINKING IN YOUR CLOSET

Clothing can come with a lot of emotional baggage, from what the size of the clothes means to you to how much money you spent on them. All of that has held you back from decluttering your closet up to this point. You're going to decide how important it is to avoid all of that emotional baggage and how important it is to feel less burdened by your clothing.

I hope you pick the latter, because the reality is that all that emotional shit is with you whether you're actively decluttering or not. It will drain you and drag you down until you take control of it all.

Limiting Beliefs: You're using your limiting beliefs as a shield so that you don't have to face the monster in your closet.

- ✕ "It will take too long to go through everything."
- ✕ "I've gotten rid of clothes before, and it didn't make that big of a difference."
- ✕ "I'll just buy more stuff, so what's the point?"

Okay, let's get real here. Just because it's going to take a chunk of time doesn't mean you can't do this. What in life that was truly important and life-changing took minimal time and effort?

If you've gone through your closet before, which we all have, you've only skimmed the surface if you didn't pull it all out and touch everything you own. This is a principle that will come up over and over. You must take everything out in order to do a thorough job of decluttering. Even then, there will probably be some stowaways that sneak back into your closet that don't need to be there. But you're going to be more aware from here on out, so you'll catch them eventually.

Fears: The boogeyman lives under your bed or in your closet. He's a manifestation of all our fears. You're going to face him down, though.

- "What if I need this someday?"
- "What if I gain/lose weight?"
- "I don't want to face those tags that point out how much weight I've gained."

Look, if you haven't yet needed that branded golf shirt you won on that outing two years ago, it's unlikely that you'll have a golf shirt emergency. If you do, there are tons of options, from brick-and-mortar stores, to online, to consignment, to secondhand shops to find a new shirt.

I had this gorgeous purple dress that I wore to two weddings one summer—and looked fabulous. Then it sat in my closet. It was unique and beautiful, and I didn't want to let it go. But I did. I still haven't had a dress emergency. I've decided that if I do, I'll go to ThredUp.com and find something secondhand.

Weight is one of the biggest fears my clients have when it comes to their clothing.

Facing the clothes that once fit but don't any longer can make you go down a rabbit hole of frustration and shame over your body. I can't solve that for you, but I will tell you that the weight you lose by getting rid of stuff that is metaphorically weighing you down can sometimes lead to actual weight loss.

Why? Because that blockage is gone. Because taking care of your home can make you feel more like taking care of yourself.

And, yes, there is the possibility that you will lose or gain weight at another time. But this is the body you have now. Live in it, accept it. Don't create a self-fulfilling prophecy by having larger clothes waiting for you as a safety net. Also, when you do lose the weight you're planning on, you might not even want the clothes you have right now.

Give yourself permission to let go.

LETTING GO OF SOME SHIT

The image I always think of for shame is that triangle-shaped closet under the stairs that a lot of old houses have: a bare bulb with a string to turn it on; the deep, dark recess at the back of the triangle where nothing actually fits. I imagine pulling shame out from that deep, dark pit and tossing it out onto the front lawn in the sun so it can wither up and die.

Maybe your shame isn't in a closet under the stairs. Maybe it's in your bedroom (and, for many, in closets throughout the house).

And then there's the perfectionist in you who doesn't want to start something you can't finish today. Or who is so paralyzed with perfectionism that you can't even look in the closet anymore so you just work from a small pile on the floor.

Shame: It's time to face the darkness inside your drawers and closet. The reason my image of shame is about taking something from the dark and tossing it into the light is that shame is all about the stuff you hide.

Clothing can be *something* to hide in.

If you don't like your body, you may wear clothes that disguise you, or you might not let yourself even buy new stuff because you feel like you don't deserve it. You'll hide yourself in the same top over and over, hoping no one will look at you.

Shame over your body won't go away as long as you keep feeding it. I had one client who had, as many did, gained a significant amount of weight over the pandemic. She loved yoga and went four times a week. But instead of feeling free and accepting of herself when she was doing yoga, which is what you hope for, she felt shame over her body and what it could no longer do.

We got to talking about this, and our conversation turned to the workout clothes she wore to class—old, faded, blown elastic, small holes, and worn fabric that all made her feel even more ashamed of her appearance.

Then she discovered Lululemon sales. All the old, ratty workout clothes were tossed and a curated and intentional collection of clothes that hugged her body in all the good ways replaced them. The smile on her face was priceless, and I wish I could bottle that shit.

Getting rid of the trappings of her old perceptions of herself made room for the clothes that gave her permission to see herself differently.

I wonder how you might see yourself if you only had clothes you loved.

Perfectionism: The largest perfectionism issue I run into is frustration over the sheer volume of clothing that needs to be addressed. Many people don't want to take my advice of going drawer to drawer, section by section. They want immediate results, and they want to get this thing done.

I don't blame you if you feel this way too. It's intimidating to consider all of the clothing the average American has.

Just think how nice it will be when you have a more intentional, curated closet of your own. You'll never have to be overwhelmed by it again.

To get there, you're going to have to let go of some shit—like the idea that you should be able to do this all-in-one. Hey, maybe you can. Maybe you have the time and space to do it in one go. Awesome! Go for it!

For the rest of you who don't: stay on task, create a plan, and get it done over time. No, it isn't instant gratification, but it will be amaze-balls once you're done.

☆ SUCCESS STRATEGY ☆

Bring in a trusted friend to hold each item up for you to make decisions on. She'll create your toss, donate, and keep piles. She can even take the toss and donate away for you. Then you can go through the keep one more time to touch everything yourself, without that initial overwhelm.

THE SHIT YOU VALUE

Your clothes and how you care for them reflect your values. Are you passionate about the planet and have mostly bamboo or other sustainable fabrics in there? Do you live for high fashion and have a closet full of designer treasures? Are you a free spirit with a boho wardrobe? Or a more restrained personality with soft colors and high necklines?

Whatever your personality, you want it to shine through in what you wear.

This is how you meet the world. You'll feel more authentic and confident if your clothes represent you properly. How awful is it to be out with friends in a top you bought because it was trendy, but all it does is make you feel like you stand out in all the wrong ways?

As you declutter, think about what you value and how your clothes represent that. Keep in mind that if you value being frugal, hanging on to things just because you spent money on them is not saving money. The money has been spent. Let the MC Hammer pants go.

The state of your clothes and your closet tell us something about how much you value yourself. Lots of holes in your T-shirts? I'm all for worn-in comfy clothes, but there's a limit. Underwear and bras with old elastic? Holes in your socks? And what does chaos in your drawers and closet say about how you treat yourself?

As you declutter, keep these things in mind.
Live authentically and value yourself.

GETTING OVER YOUR SHITTY HABITS

Oh, I know you're rockin' some crappy clothing habits.

- You pile them up on that chair in the corner that was meant for reading.
- You drop them on the floor outside your closet because it's too much trouble to go inside your closet.
- You're overwhelmed by laundry and never fold anything, so you live out of laundry baskets.
- You somehow manage to drop your dirty clothes around the hamper instead of in it.

- When a stack of clothes on a shelf in your closet tips over, you shove it back into place instead of refolding and restacking.
- You dress out of the laundry room.
- You aren't sure anymore what's clean and what's dirty, so you end up washing it all over again.

Decide how you're going to do shit differently moving forward. No more living like a drunk raccoon got into your closet. Whatever the shitty habit is, work yourself backwards to figure out what you need to avoid doing in the first place so the old habit never even has a chance.

Let's say you have a hamper in your room filled with clothing that has slowly built up over time, and you don't even know what's in the basket anymore.

STEP 1: Ask yourself how this happened. "When I don't know what to do with something or don't have time, I drop it in the hamper."

STEP 2: Ask yourself how you can avoid this in the future. "I can't have a catch-all hamper in the first place. I need to have systems in place so I'll know where to put things, and it won't take hardly any time to put them away."

You have to be honest with yourself. If you say in this scenario that you need to stop dropping crap in the hamper, that probably won't be enough. If that was all it took, you would have done it a long time ago. You have to set yourself up for success with new systems that are realistic and take your personality into account.

☆ SUCCESS STRATEGY ☆

Try using a folding board to speed up flat-folding shirts.

LET'S SET THE SHIT OUT OF SOME GOALS!

You can easily get overwhelmed by the sheer volume of clothing you have. You might think you don't really have all that much, but I'm guessing you have enough to wear a different outfit for a year without repeating a combination. After decluttering, I took inventory and found that I had around 250 items of clothing, not including underthings or shoes. I currently have about 35 pairs of shoes. When I started, I had approximately double that, and I am painfully aware that my wardrobe was nothing in comparison to many. Decide how you want to start.

- **Small Victory:** Declutter one drawer.
- **Big Impact:** Clear out that pile in the corner so you can actually see the floor and use the chair under the mess.
- **Irritant:** Finally take that bag of to-be-donated clothes you put together months ago and never followed through on.
- **Worst:** Dive into your closet and show that clutter who's boss!

If you're going to do this all in one day, or even in one week, it's going to take a lot of time and energy. If you're going to spread it out over time, it's going to take consistency and re-upping your motivation now and then. What will that look like? Be honest and realistic.

THE TAKEAWAY

Your clothes represent who you are or who you see yourself to be. They can come with a lot of emotional baggage. Don't let yourself get derailed by that emotion. Create a realistic plan to get through everything. Be gentle with yourself when you're facing that emotion. With each chunk you declutter, create a new system that will keep it that way.

You wear your clothes, not the other way around.

MAKING IT REAL

Now that you've worked on yourself, and you've reviewed the process of decluttering your clothes, it's time to check in, get honest, and create a plan.

Before you declutter your clothes, answer these questions.

What do you feel when you think about decluttering your clothes? Check all that apply: ☐ **Angry** ☐ **Hopeless** ☐ **Anxious** ☐ **Joyful** ☐ **Ashamed** ☐ **Loving** ☐ **Doubtful** ☐ **Overwhelmed** ☐ **Excited** ☐ **Sad** ☐ **Hopeful** ☐ **Other** ________	How would you like to feel about your clothes? Please describe:
What Stage of Change do you see yourself in when you think about your clothes? (*See Chapter 1.*) Why?	If you haven't reached Action, what do you think you need to do to move into the next stage? (*See Chapter 1.*)
What limiting beliefs have kept you from decluttering your clothes? (*See Chapter 2.*)	What fears do you have about beginning to declutter your clothes? (*See Chapter 2.*)
If you are feeling shame, describe what about your clothes makes you feel there is something wrong with you. (*See Chapter 3.*)	If you are dealing with perfectionism, how is that holding you back from taking care of your clothes? (*See Chapter 3.*)
How are your values either shown or attacked in your clothes? (*See Chapter 4.*)	What habits have led to the clutter in your clothes? (*See Chapter 5.*)
What are your top five goals for your clothes? (*See Chapter 6.*) **1.** **2.** **3.** **4.** **5.**	What steps will you take to reach those goals? (*See Chapter 6.*) **1.** **2.** **3.** **4.** **5.**

CLOTHING CHECKLIST

☐ Sweaters	☐ Workout Clothes	☐ Scarves	☐ Long Sleeves
☐ Hats	☐ Dresses	☐ Jackets	☐ Short Sleeves
☐ Socks	☐ Dress Pants	☐ Blouses	☐ T-Shirts
☐ Underthings	☐ Ties	☐ Casual Pants	☐ Bathing Suits
☐ Jeans	☐ Tank Tops	☐ Shorts	☐ Cover-Ups
☐ Shoes	☐ Skirts	☐ Leggings	☐ Sweatshirts

After you have decluttered your clothes, come back and answer these questions.

How do you feel when you think about your clothing now?

What new habits will you be putting in place to maintain your clothes?

Do you have any new goals for your clothes since decluttering?

CHAPTER 13

SHIT STILL EXISTS, EVEN IF YOU HIDE IT!

I didn't have a garage until I moved into the house I live in now. What I did have when I was a kid was a big red barn. Yup. The sort of thing you see in movies. But this barn wasn't housing cows and sheep and stuff. It was just housing stuff.

Yes, at one point we did have two horses and a bunch of pet pigeons, but the rest of the barn was filled with the belongings of generations of people we didn't even know. My sisters and I would climb around in there (not exactly safe, but hey, it was the '70s) and found things like original Barbies—the ones with the blond ponytail. Why were they in a barn? No clue. Barns are weird. If only we had understood what her collector value would be decades later. Alas, we were simply kids climbing around in a barn finding toys.

I have come to learn garages, basements, and sheds are just as weird as our barn was. I now voyeuristically peek at people's garages when I pass them to see what's in there. How do they use their garage? For car storage, as a man cave, for the storage of everything ever, possibly including the Ark of the Covenant?

☆ SUCCESS STRATEGY ☆

Only fill any area of your home to a maximum 80 percent capacity.

As for basements, the one we had when I was a kid had stuff in it, but it was a dirt basement, so it really wasn't meant for living like the basements of other people I knew. It was good for hanging out every time the sky turned green and my mother hustled us down there, convinced a good Midwestern tornado was about to take us to Oz (it never did get that exciting).

As an adult, I always wanted a basement. I coveted the finished basements my friends had with TVs and bars. Then I decluttered and thanked my lucky stars we had never pushed for a bigger home with that basement we wanted when we first bought this house, and that we had never bothered to upsize like we were so sure we would someday.

It's like a purse. The bigger the house, the more crap you stuff in it.

THINGS THAT MAKE YOU GO HMMM . . .

HARD TRUTHS NO ONE WANTS ME TO TELL THEM.

I'm going to get a bit tough here. It isn't out of judgment or frustration with you. It's because I've been doing the work I do with people for a long damn time, and the only way I can do my job is because there are certain simple truths and consistencies with human beings. That all means: I know what I'm talking about. All your what-ifs are sweet and naive, but here's the truth.

If your kids have a healthy relationship with stuff, they are not going to want their old toys for their children.	Your daughter is not going to want your old clothes when she grows to be the same size as you in another ten years.	Those CDs and VHS tapes are not going to be worth something someday.
Holding on to the stuff you used in a former life/job is not how you stop time.	You're never going to use all those cords. You don't even know what half of them go to.	That T-shirt collection of your deceased husband's will mold and rot away. Find a purpose for it to honor him.
Grandma is not going to step down from heaven to chastise you for getting rid of her stuff.	You are not going to suddenly get a bee up your ass and fix all of those broken things you've stored away.	That furniture you have in a storage unit that you didn't have a use for, but thought it'd be a waste to get rid of? You're never going to use it.
If you've taken the time to put clothes into bins, then put them away in a storage area and haven't taken them out in over two years, you aren't going to use them.	Unless you're going to be moving soon, as in this year, saving cardboard boxes is only taking up space. Recycle them now.	Decluttering does not mean putting stuff in boxes and then putting them in the basement.

WELL, SHIT, AM I READY FOR THIS?

Thinking about how ready you are to tackle storage areas will probably depend on the space you're talking about.

- Basement
- Attic
- Garage
- Catch-all closet
- Crawl space
- Shed
- Storage locker
- Any other sneaky place you've shoved stuff

As you ask yourself about your readiness, have a specific storage space in mind. You might be happy to turn the attic from creepy to creative. Or you might wish you were ready to take care of your basement but simply can't get yourself motivated.

- **Precontemplation:** "If I just get another storage locker, this won't be a problem."
- **Contemplation:** "I would love to clear out the shed and those storage lockers, but it seems so overwhelming."
- **Preparation:** "I gotta do this. Things are getting ruined, mice are crawling on stuff, and there's a strange smell coming from in there."
- **Action:** "I'm glad we got that dumpster! So much of this is just garbage. I can't wait to turn this space into my new yoga studio."
- **Maintenance:** "These storage spaces are not for things I don't know what to do with. They stay nice and organized because I now actually know what's in there."

Remember, there's a reason these areas get out of control: out of sight, out of mind. If you're thinking about the space now, it might be a good idea to get going on it because once you put it in the back of your head, it may be another year before you think of it again.

SHITTY THINKING IN YOUR STORAGE AREAS

The limiting beliefs and fears you have around your storage spaces will vary depending on the space, and the crap in it. You might even have different categories in a single space. You might be totally fine with one category, but thinking about that other stuff in there may stop you from dealing with anything.

Limiting Beliefs: When you're dealing with storage spaces that are overrun with goodness knows what, your limiting beliefs will probably be along the lines of not believing in your ability to face it down or get it done.

"There's just too much crap in there. There's no way I'll be able to get through it all."

I've had clients get dumpsters so they can go through their garages. I've had others go to their storage locker(s) every Saturday until the job was done. Others have set aside vacation time to tackle an overrun basement or garage. Remember Katie and her summer vacation garage makeover?

It does take planning, but you can totally get through it all. And I'll tell you that a cleared-out storage space gives an immense sense of satisfaction when it's done, because it's such a big area and has such a large impact.

Fears: Large, often dark spaces, filled with decades of cast-off crap? What's to fear in there? Ah, yes, lots of stuff.

- ✕ "Ew, I don't want to find out what's under all of that."
- ✕ "I'm afraid I won't want to get rid of anything."
- ✕ "I don't know if I'm up to the task."

Look, there is absolutely the possibility that you will find moldy items, mouse droppings, mouse nests, earwigs, cockroaches, and any other horrors you can think of. That's what face masks, rubber gloves, etc., are for. I've been there. I've done that. You can too.

You have to ask yourself if you'd rather avoid the task and continue to live knowing there could be ick under all of that stuff, or suck it up and git 'er done.

Do not worry, you will want to get rid of stuff. You'll want to get rid of a lot of stuff. We're talking about spaces that have been neglected for years. Crap has piled up in there that you haven't missed all these years. You'll be relieved to get rid of it.

A big space filled with piles of things and boxes of mysteries can be intimidating. You look at it and you have no idea where to start, so you think you can't start. Here's what you do:

STEP 1: Stand in front of the chaos. Stare it down and tell it you're the one in charge. Think "Mr. Mom triumphing over the vacuum"-type energy.

STEP 2: Pick something up. Anything. It does not matter. You're going to get to it all eventually, so it really doesn't matter what you start with.

STEP 3: Make a decision. If you can't make a decision, put it aside.

STEP 4: Repeat until you've touched everything.

You'll be amazed at what you can accomplish when you take control, rather than focusing on the fear.

LETTING GO OF SOME SHIT

You're taking control. You're the one in charge, not fear or your limiting beliefs. You're feeling strong and confident. Then you stand in front of that pile and shame sweeps over you.

You feel gross and bad for being someone who has let a space get this out of control. Just facing it makes you kinda want to throw up.

Then you re-read the instructions on facing fear and starting with one thing at a time. You take a deep breath and wrangle your shame. Then your inner perfectionist raises your head and freezes you in place.

Excuses start to flow, and another day goes by during which you don't accomplish what you wanted to, and you get to feel even worse about yourself. It's time to change that.

It's time to face the demons hiding at the back of that giant pile of stuff and do this.

Shame: The storage spaces that you toss things into willy-nilly, then slam the door shut so you don't have to look at it, are the epitome of shame—dark hidden places you never show anyone. I've talked about this, though, haven't I? You have to drag stuff out of the deep recesses and expose them to the light so that your shame can melt away.

Open that door and give yourself permission to face the shame and chaos.

Give yourself permission to stop torturing yourself and find out you are not bad because you let stuff pile up. It's just stuff. It has nothing to do with your worth.

Perfectionism: Your inner perfectionist cringes at the sight of this much mayhem. You're afraid to start. You're afraid that once you start, you'll do it wrong. You think it all has to be done in one day, and you're totally overwhelmed.

All I can tell you, over and over, is that you have to take the risk to start, take the risk of doing it wrong. If you don't, then your perfectionism becomes the excuse to never gain control of your home and your space. Then fuck it, you might as well burn this book, curl up in a ball, and give up.

No? That's not what you're going to do? Excellent!

Look, sometimes you can do these things in one day, if you truly have the time and energy. One couple got their entire garage done in two days because that was how long they had rented the dumpster for. They couldn't stop because of all the mouse evidence or soggy cardboard and ruined items. They had to keep forging forward.

But if you don't have that kind of deadline, you can do this in stages. You're going to set your goals, and then you're going to figure out how to get those goals attained.

You'll have a plan. Trust in the plan. Have faith in yourself. Faith is believing in something you have no evidence of. From faith can come trust in yourself.

Let go and trust.

THE SHIT YOU VALUE

Did you ever watch the show *American Pickers*? Well, it's a show with two guys who own an antiques shop and go around the country poking through people's garages, barns, attics, etc., to see if there are any treasures hiding in the chaos that they can buy from the owners.

They open the door to something like a small barn, and it would be wall-to-wall, floor-to-ceiling stuff. So much that you can't even pick out what's in there. The guys push on through, often climbing on things to get to a treasure they see peeking out from the trash.

The interesting and confounding thing was the number of items people had shoved in these spaces, where no one would ever see them or use them—that they refused to part with, no matter how much they were offered.

Here's my thing: If you truly value something, you don't treat it like trash. You also don't shove it in a dark space to never be seen again.

I had one client who had moved into a new house where there wasn't enough room for everything, and it was making things very difficult for her.

She mentioned boxes with books in them. When we talked about what to do with them, she admitted that these particular books had been in boxes for about fifteen years. Which meant they had already been in boxes for about ten years before her divorce and four subsequent moves that landed her in this house with her new husband.

As we talked about these books, it became clear she was

holding on to them, not because she loved them, but because she felt it made her look smart or educated to have them. Remember, the books had never been out for anyone else to see, so no one had ever had a chance to judge her as smart or educated based on the presence of these books.

This was a feeling that stemmed back to her family, and their values that she felt she had to live up to.

She had a college education and had worked as a nurse for over twenty years at this point. On the outside, she already looked smart and educated to observers.

In the end, she divorced her second husband and finally moved to Florida, which she had wanted to do for years. In doing this, she decided it was the end of the road for those books. They no longer represented the values of her family of origin to her, but rather the relationships with narcissistic men that had held her back for so long. She was breaking free in so many ways, and those boxes of books had no place in her new freedom. She had finally decided she valued herself above all that other crap.

The shit you store may say a hell of a lot more about what you think you should value, rather than what you really *do* value.

GETTING OVER YOUR SHITTY HABITS

Keeping the idea of what you actually value versus what you think you should value in mind, what habits have you developed over the years that have led to that storage space you keep stuffed to the gills?

Do you keep boxing up each year of your kids' school assignments and art projects? Do you throw crap into the garage so you don't have to deal with it and can move on to the next life event?

Are you storing furniture in a storage locker for a house you may never own? Have you been collecting something because you're convinced it will be valuable someday and you'll be able to make money off it? (That rarely works out, BTW.)

Shoving things into storage spaces without an organizational system, let alone a plan, will cost you more time and aggravation later on.

It's a problem a lot of us have: using a shortcut makes today easier but makes tomorrow ten times harder.

Stop it. Really, just stop. Think. How much time will it really take you to put that thing away with intention? Do you really need to keep that thing? If you're going to put that thing in your hand into a box, will it come out again? Seriously, be honest with yourself.

After you declutter, create systems and rules that will keep these spaces looking as beautiful on day 365 as they do on day one.

LET'S SET THE SHIT OUT OF SOME GOALS!

Storage spaces can be the most intimidating and overwhelming areas of your home. They tend to be big spaces with little to no organizational sectioning. The years of shoving stuff in them without worrying about the growing chaos comes back to bite you in the ass.

But even the biggest, most overwhelming space can be dealt with as long as you have a plan. Decide what you want to start with, even if it's just one little item, and go from there.

- **Small Victory:** One small box of crap.
- **Big Impact:** If you can get to them, removing large furniture items.
- **Irritant:** Getting rid of that thing you always trip over or that falls on you every time you attempt to get into the storage space.
- **Worst:** That pile of boxes that somehow got waterlogged and you have no idea if anything in them is salvageable.

Wherever you choose to start, you also want to have an idea as to where you want to end. There are going to be a lot of starts and stops before you get to the final ending. The big finale might be to have the space totally empty, or it might be to have the ability to create an art space here or get storage racks with clear bins for everything.

But you have to start at the beginning. Thinking too hard about that finale might make it all feel impossible. What is the first starting and ending you want to focus on?

If it's one small box of crap, your beginning might be:

- Pull the box out and open it up.

Your end might be:

- Have an empty box to put donations in.
- Be able to burn or recycle all of the papers from the box.
- Have a pile for each of your kids to take.

Whatever your start or end is, remember to make it realistic for the time and energy you have. You don't have to overachieve. If you have a full day to dig in, go for it. If you have fifteen minutes to get something done, look at your plan and decide what you can do that will leave you feeling like you accomplished *something*, instead of having opened a can of worms that you have to leave open because you have somewhere to be.

One start and end at a time, you will get through this. There is an end, I promise. This space is finite. It has walls and can only hold so much. Don't give up, even if you're frustrated that the project you thought you could do in one day is really a three-week project. You get to choose if your mindset is frustration or "hell yeah!"

"Hell yeah" is the one that will keep you going so you get to feel amazing once you've reached your goal.

THE TAKEAWAY

Storage spaces are sneaky little fuckers. They are prone to getting filled with the odds and ends of life that you don't want to deal with.

No one wants to tackle storage. Closets and kitchens are the sexy places to declutter and organize.

That being said, the feeling of achievement when you've cleared a space that looked impossible when you started is worth all your time and energy.

Because they're out of sight/out of mind, storage spaces don't seem like they could be draining you every day. But you know that space exists, even if you aren't looking at it all the time. In the back of your head, you always know it's there, and that's what drains you.

Free yourself from the draining grip of storage. Declutter, organize, and move on.

MAKING IT REAL

Now that you've worked on yourself, and you've reviewed the process of decluttering your storage spaces, it's time to check in, get honest, and create a plan.

Before you declutter each storage space, answer these questions.

<table>
<tr>
<td>What do you feel when you think about decluttering this storage space? Check all that apply:
☐ Angry ☐ Hopeless ☐ Anxious
☐ Joyful ☐ Ashamed ☐ Loving
☐ Doubtful ☐ Overwhelmed ☐ Excited
☐ Sad ☐ Hopeful ☐ Other __________</td>
<td>How would you like to feel about this storage space? Please describe:</td>
</tr>
<tr>
<td>What Stage of Change do you see yourself in when you think about this storage space? (See Chapter 1.) Why?</td>
<td>If you haven't reached Action, what do you think you need to do to move into the next stage? (See Chapter 1.)</td>
</tr>
<tr>
<td>What limiting beliefs have kept you from decluttering this storage space? (See Chapter 2.)</td>
<td>What fears do you have about beginning to declutter this storage space? (See Chapter 2.)</td>
</tr>
<tr>
<td>If you are feeling shame, describe what about this storage space makes you feel there is something wrong with you. (See Chapter 3.)</td>
<td>If you are dealing with perfectionism, how is that holding you back from taking care of this storage space? (See Chapter 3.)</td>
</tr>
<tr>
<td>How are your values either shown or attacked in this storage space? (See Chapter 4.)</td>
<td>What habits have led to the clutter in this storage space? (See Chapter 5.)</td>
</tr>
<tr>
<td>What are your top five goals for this storage space? (See Chapter 6.)
1.
2.
3.
4.
5.</td>
<td>What steps will you take to reach those goals? (See Chapter 6.)
1.
2.
3.
4.
5.</td>
</tr>
</table>

STORAGE SPACE CHECKLIST

☐ Closets	☐ Garage	☐ M-in-Law Cottage
☐ Attic	☐ Above the Garage	☐ Greenhouse
☐ Basement	☐ Barn	☐ Boathouse
☐ Crawl Spaces	☐ Old Trailer	☐ Old Chicken Coop
☐ Shed	☐ Studio	☐ Pool House
☐ Storage Locker	☐ Extra Rooms	☐ Parents' House

After you have decluttered your storage space, come back and answer these questions.

How do you feel when you think about this storage space now?

What new habits will you be putting in place to maintain this storage space?

Do you have any new goals for this storage space since decluttering?

CHAPTER 14

SENTIMENTAL SHIT

I once had a client, Kristin, say something that I thought at the time was one of the strangest things ever: "I know it's weird to keep something just because I love it."

When she said this, I didn't understand what she meant. In my thinking, the only things you keep are the things that you love. What I came to understand she was referring to was *sentimental clutter.*

That moment made me realize it's important for me to say it's okay to hold on to things that have no other value than sentiment.

If something has wonderful memories attached to it and is something that you really love having, that's exactly the stuff that you want to keep.

As Kristin and I continued to talk, I realized we needed

to differentiate between what was clutter and what were mementos.

Mementos are things that are held sacred and taken care of. Perhaps they're displayed. Perhaps they are kept in cedar boxes that ward off moths.

Clutter is the stuff you call collections and mementos that you think are your memories but are really the odds and ends filling drawers and shelves in corners, dragging all of your energy down.

Think about it for a moment. Think about one thing you have in your home that is a memento from a wonderful time in your life or reminds you of a loved one. Think about how you care for that item. Is it displayed? Do you know exactly where it is? Is it dusted off? Is it loved?

Now go ahead and think about something that you have that, in your heart of hearts, you know is clutter. This is something that you probably keep out of a sense of guilt or obligation.

Notice how differently you feel when you think about each of these items. This is how you can tell the difference between a memento that is loved and to be kept and sentimental clutter that is just getting in the way.

In my own home, I have a small rock collection from places Shawn and I have traveled—Peru, Iceland, the Colosseum in Rome, Tahiti, the Giant's Causeway in Northern Ireland, and so on. I have these displayed on the shelf above my yoga mat in my office. I also have the shirts we were both wearing the night we met at the Goth dance club Neo in Chicago on June 5, 1998, wrapped in tissue in a box in my closet.

I care for these items and hold them dear, for no other reason than that it gives me the warm fuzzies to have them.

In moderation, sentimentality can have its place in your home.

THINGS THAT MAKE YOU GO HMMM . . .

But what am I supposed to do with these precious things?

For almost everything else you declutter, you'll be willing to toss it or donate it. Some stuff you'll want to sell because it's worth something and worth the effort to you.

With sentimental stuff, it gets a little trickier as to what to do with it all. Here are a few ideas to help get you unstuck.

Take photos of things before you let them go. It's like taking steps. Eventually you'll delete the photo because you won't need it, but for now you'll have the picture to look back on.	***Repurpose items***. I had a client whose husband had died and left 10, no kidding, 10 boxes of Harley-Davidson T-shirts. A year after his passing, she had a quilt made for everyone in the family.
If you don't want to deal with selling, ask a friend who does Poshmark, Facebook Marketplace, or eBay to sell your stuff for you for a cut of the profits.	***Send a message out to family members*** that as of X date you'll be donating all of X stuff. If anyone wants any of it, they can come get it. Don't be hurt if they don't want it, though.
Donate clothes to a women's shelter. They most often need underthings and socks, but they may be open to clothes, especially if they're larger sizes.	***Talk to antique shops*** in the area about buying items if you feel that's appropriate.
Artwork is really hard. I was raised by artists. Again, tell people to come get it by a certain time. Or, as my artist mother said once, it's okay to not be so precious about it.	***Know someone setting up their first home?*** Give them the option to rummage through stuff.
Have an estate sale. There are people who will help you set that up. It doesn't have to only be after someone has passed away.	***In the end***, if you have to tuck some things into boxes with a reminder in your phone to go back in and look at the stuff every 3 months, that's okay too.

WELL, SHIT, AM I READY FOR THIS?

Human beings love symbolism. Sentimental clutter is all about symbolism. To be ready to dive into your sentimental stuff, you have to know what it symbolizes for you. Then you'll be more able to decide whether you can let it go or not.

For example, that vase that belonged to your grandma that's really pretty, but isn't your style at all, but you can't seem to part with it? It symbolizes your grandma. Letting go of the vase isn't letting go of her. Now that you know why you're keeping it, you can decide if you would like to let go of it, or if you want to display it somewhere to remind you of her.

As you try to figure out what things symbolize, you'll sort through your Stages of Change as always.

- **Precontemplation:** "I can't get rid of any of this stuff. These are memories. I'd feel lost without it all."
- **Contemplation:** "I'm starting to realize I never look at or use any of this. Maybe I could live without all of this."
- **Preparation:** "I've got a plan. I don't have to get rid of everything, but I know I'll feel lighter if I let go of the past."
- **Action:** "I remember when we went on this trip. That was so much fun. I guess I don't need this souvenir, because I've never even used it. I'll just revel in the memories on my own."
- **Maintenance:** "It's so nice displaying the most important things that were in there. And there's even space for a few more really important things to join the rest."

Sentimental crap that clogs up your home holds you back and needs to go. Sentimental symbols displayed or used properly can honor sacred memories. Which one are you ready to do?

I'll be totally honest with you: When we downsize our home, there is a huge likelihood that a rock collection and two shirts that live in a closet won't make the cut. Decluttering taught me to know I can hold on to my sentimental crap, but I can also live without it because my life is what's happening right now.

SHITTY THINKING IN YOUR SENTIMENTS

When you're staring sentimental clutter in the face, you might find yourself feeling incredibly guilty, as if getting rid of this stuff is hurting someone else.

That's what guilt is: the belief and fear that you're *hurting someone* else by getting rid of stuff. Shame is when you believe you're *bad* for getting rid of stuff. Try to keep those two separate.

Limiting Beliefs: The idea that you're harming someone else by getting rid of a thing is a major limiting belief of sentimental clutter.

Look, if someone else is butt-hurt over you reducing clutter in your home by getting rid of something they gave you, that's their problem. You thinking it's your problem is your limiting belief. You deserve to clear your space and let go of crap that drains you or holds you back.

Another limiting belief you might run into is that you'll lose the memory if you let go of the stuff. If that's the case, then those must not be very important memories, which then begs the question of why the hell you're clinging to them.

Go back and figure out the symbolism, then let go.

Fears: You're afraid people will be angry with you if you don't keep this stuff, afraid your kids will be angry and hurt that you didn't keep bins and bins of their childhood crap.

Most adults don't want to be burdened by their childhood; stop putting that on them. You're the one clinging. Don't make excuses that have to do with other people. If keeping all of those bins makes you feel closer to your kids, fine: keep them. But you may want to look at your relationship with them if you need stuff to feel close to them.

> **☆ SUCCESS STRATEGY ☆**
>
> **Ask your kids if they want all this stuff you're holding on to. They're going to say no 99 percent of the time. For the 1 percent who say yes, you can create a plan to give them the stuff. Just make sure you don't sacrifice your space and energy because of their fear of letting go.**

LETTING GO OF SOME SHIT

Sentimentality might not seem like it would lend itself to perfectionism and shame. But these are sneaky issues, and they'll jump up and bite you in the ass if you don't dig them out.

Shame: As soon as you feel like you have to hide the fact that you're getting rid of sentimental items, that's your warning sign that you're feeling ashamed. But what is this shame about? Are you supposed to feel badly about yourself because you decided your present comfort in your home is more important than mementos from a past that has come and gone?

Your shame is probably more about your relationships with other people than it is about the stuff you're wanting to let go of.

Perfectionism: Black-and-white, all-or-nothing thinking is what gets you into trouble with perfectionism. The idea that, if you let go of sentimental items, you'll lose the memories or feelings that go with them, is pretty all-or-nothing. The idea that you have to keep everything you inherited from your grandma, or all of your kids' elementary school art projects, is pretty black-and-white thinking.

Moderation is where you find the most peace.

Instead of being owned by these sentimental things, you get to enjoy them because you don't feel suffocated by them. Find the middle ground. You don't have to get rid of everything to prove you're a good declutterer, but you also don't have to keep everything to prove you're a good parent, adult child, grandparent, grandchild, aunt/uncle, best friend, sibling, etc.

THE SHIT YOU VALUE

You value things like memories and experiences. These are wonderful things to value. But at what point does your interpretation of how you're supposed to express those values start clogging up your home?

Shawn and I travel a lot. We love to explore different parts of the world with different languages and cultures. While doing this, we take a shit ton of pictures. Back when we had to haul around 35mm film, we were way more selective about what we took pictures of. Now that it's all digital, my fingers just keep tapping the shutter button over and over.

When we went to Tahiti for ten days, I came back with over 4,000 pictures. Half of them were underwater from the amazing lagoon our bungalow was in. I printed about 1,200 of those pictures and put them into four photo albums. Do you know how much room that takes up!?

I don't need all of those pictures to remind me of how amazing that trip was. Since then, I've made a photo book through Walgreens that takes up maybe five percent of the space those photo albums took up. The best pictures went in there, and that's all we need.

☆ SUCCESS STRATEGY ☆

Use online services to create photo books or scrapbooks as quick flip-throughs of special times in your life that you want to be able to revisit through photos.

My father was a photographer for most of my childhood, so I grew up with a camera in my hand. I value photography and art very highly. That doesn't mean I have to keep every picture I ever take, though. It means I can decide what's worth keeping and what isn't.

You have to reconcile all of your values.

If you value space, you're going to have to figure out how you can honor the other things you value like memories, while giving yourself permission to have that space.

GETTING OVER YOUR SHITTY HABITS

When it comes to sentimentality, the shittiest habit is keeping things:

- ✕ Just because.
- ✕ Out of fear of upsetting someone else.

Do you keep vacation souvenirs that you never use "just because" that was a great trip? Or maybe you keep your kids' school stuff "just because" it's from their lives. Heck, you might even keep things "just because" you always have.

"Just because" is never going to be a good enough reason. Be intentional. If you're keeping that souvenir, ask yourself:

1. **Why** is this particular thing worthy of staying?
2. **What** is the purpose?
3. **When** are you actually going to use or appreciate this thing?
4. **Where** has this been living all this time, and **where** do you really want it to go?

Be curious about yourself and your habits. Just because something was a gift or is attached to a memory isn't enough.

Look, this is coming from someone who has been keeping memory books since I met my husband in 1998. Receipts, tickets, vacation itineraries, wristbands, etc. Over time, my criteria for things to go in the books have gotten more specific. It was once anything and everything paper from any experience we had. Now it's select items that trigger those happy memories that we can look through together as we get older. There's value in that for me.

That brings us to the fear of upsetting other people. You are given gifts and inherit things now and then. You don't always want these things; but instead of saying "no, thank you," you take them knowing they're going to the bottom of a drawer or out to the garage in a bin.

It isn't always comfortable to say no to things people want to give you, but it's a heck of a lot more honest.

If other people think you're being rude by not taking the thing, that's their issue they need to work through. They're assigning personal meaning to your "no" and deciding they're supposed to be affronted.

Other people will get it, and, even if they're disappointed, they'll be accepting of your boundary.

My very sweet and very well-meaning father-in-law once gave me a pair of shoes for my birthday. He knew I liked shoes. He knew I had a lot of black shoes. He knew I liked heels. But clothing can be a very personal thing, and these shoes, while being cute, were simply something I would never wear.

Right there in the restaurant where we were having a small birthday dinner, I said, "Thank you; however, I won't wear these, so I'll need to return them." He was disappointed but accepted it. I didn't go home with shoes I felt obligated to keep or to wear in his presence. That was the last time he tried to buy me something personal like that. Instead, he takes me to dinner and watches our cats when we're away. The cat thing is all I need. The dinner thing is a bonus.

Saying yes to things you don't want is another shitty habit to get past. It just complicates things. Declutter your life by cutting out the unnecessary obligations.

Keep the things that you want, love, and use. Let the rest go. You do not have to be dragged down by obligations, and you certainly don't need a house full of mementos no one ever sees.

LET'S SET THE SHIT OUT OF SOME GOALS!

Let's move some of this sentimental crap out. As with everything else, you might feel overwhelmed by volume or by feelings. Start wherever is most comfortable for you.

- **Small Victory:** Those candlesticks you got for your wedding because you were so sure you were going to have romantic candlelit dinners with your honey, but decided the spilled wax wasn't worth it.
- **Big Impact:** The giant china hutch you got from your aunt that fit in your old house but doesn't fit in your current house.
- **Irritant:** All those shot glasses from your adventures that you rarely use yet have piled up over the years. And when you do use them, you never need *that* many.
- **Worst:** The bins of your kids' stuff stacked in the basement that you keep saying you're going to go through, but it never happens because it has felt way too overwhelming before now.

Starting with a small victory can help boost your confidence that this isn't really as awful as you thought it was going to be. Getting an irritant out can feel like you finally scratched an itch. Tackling the worst or biggest things can feel like you accomplished something major, and if you can do this, you can do anything!

Be gentle with yourself, though. In setting your goals, keep your emotional self in mind. Sentimental shit can bring up a lot of feelings.

Go slow if you need to. Be very sure you're ready to get rid of these things. For the most part, they are not things you can replace, like most of the stuff in the rest of the house. Once sentimental stuff is gone, it isn't coming back.

I've had clients get rid of things they weren't ready to get rid of because they thought they were supposed to be ready, and then they regretted it. This set their decluttering back significantly because they were now more fearful of making a mistake.

Go back to your Stages of Change.
Be honest with yourself as to where you are.

If you aren't ready to take action on something, put it back and move on to something else. This crap has been here for a while; if it has to stick around for a little longer, it won't kill anyone. At least now you've been reminded that it's there, and that will help you come back to it at a later date when you've processed it a bit more.

THE TAKEAWAY

Sentimentality can be sweet: things that tickle your senses and take you back to a special time in your life. A smell, a sound, a flavor, an image, or texture like sand between your toes, these are things that bring those memories forward.

Knickknacks that collect dust are not sacred symbols of special times. Things kept in boxes in your garage or basement are not helping keep memories alive.

How do you know what is truly special if you keep everything?

Being selective is how you determine the specialness of any of your belongings, but especially the ones tied to the past. If everything is jumbled together or stuffed away in boxes, how are you supposed to enjoy those special things?

Give your memories a special place by being selective with the mementos you keep.

MAKING IT REAL

Now that you've worked on yourself, and you've reviewed the process of decluttering your sentimental stuff, it's time to check in, get honest, and create a plan.

Before you declutter your sentimental stuff, answer these questions.

What do you feel when you think about decluttering your sentimental stuff? Check all that apply: ☐ **Angry** ☐ **Hopeless** ☐ **Anxious** ☐ **Joyful** ☐ **Ashamed** ☐ **Loving** ☐ **Doubtful** ☐ **Overwhelmed** ☐ **Excited** ☐ **Sad** ☐ **Hopeful** ☐ **Other** ___________	How would you like to feel about your sentimental stuff? Please describe:
What Stage of Change do you see yourself in when you think about your sentimental stuff? (*See Chapter 1.*) Why?	If you haven't reached Action, what do you think you need to do to move into the next stage? (*See Chapter 1.*)
What limiting beliefs have kept you from decluttering your sentimental stuff? (*See Chapter 2.*)	What fears do you have about beginning to declutter your sentimental stuff? (*See Chapter 2.*)
If you are feeling shame, describe what about your sentimental stuff makes you feel there is something wrong with you. (*See Chapter 3.*)	If you are dealing with perfectionism, how is that holding you back from taking care of your sentimental stuff? (*See Chapter 3.*)
How are your values either shown or attacked in your sentimental stuff? (*See Chapter 4.*)	What habits have led to the clutter in your sentimental stuff? (*See Chapter 5.*)
What are your top five goals for your sentimental stuff? (*See Chapter 6.*) **1.** **2.** **3.** **4.** **5.**	What steps will you take to reach those goals? (*See Chapter 6.*) **1.** **2.** **3.** **4.** **5.**

SENTIMENTAL STUFF CHECKLIST

☐ Souvenirs	☐ College Items	☐ Photographs	☐ Wedding Dress
☐ Inherited Items	☐ Old-Life Items	☐ Old Letters	☐ Varsity Jacket
☐ Special Clothes	☐ Gifts	☐ Kids' Artwork	☐ Collections
☐ Baby Clothes	☐ Old Journals	☐ College Textbooks	☐ Knickknacks
☐ Old Toys	☐ Wedding Items	☐ Old Jewelry	☐ Heirlooms
☐ Bridal Bouquet	☐ Ornaments	☐ Mementos	☐ Scrapbooks

After you have decluttered your sentimental stuff, come back and answer these questions.

How do you feel when you think about your sentimental stuff now?

What new habits will you be putting in place to maintain your sentimental stuff?

Do you have any new goals for your sentimental stuff since decluttering?

CONCLUSION: WHAT THE ACTUAL SHIT!? YOU DID IT!

Damn! I'm so fucking proud of you. You were scared, you doubted the process, you hung in there, and you gave yourself the gift of deciding you are worth having a home you feel joyful in.

Your heart is lighter, your mind is free, your home is clear, and energy is flowing. You've done good work!

There's just a little bit more I have to tell you about: sustainability.

In this chapter, I'll sum up your work and talk about what it takes to sustain your new systems and keep adjusting as needed over time.

This was just the beginning. But what a glorious beginning it has been, and I can't wait to see what the ripple effect is going to be into your entire life from here.

Hell, yeah!

WHAT YOU'VE LEARNED ABOUT YOURSELF

You've kicked ass and taken names for the sake of creating real change in your life and home. As a recap, in case you didn't realize how much you've done up to now, here's what you've learned:

- **Stages of Change:** You now know how to look at a situation and figure out whether you're ready for change or if you still need to do some work to get yourself there.
- **Thoughts:** You can identify a limiting belief and the fears those beliefs come from so you can overcome them.
- **Attachments:** You can tell when perfectionism and shame are trying to take over, counter them, and decide on your own criteria for what you will or will not hold on to.
- **Values:** You have a greater understanding of what you value and how that translates into an uncluttered life and home.
- **Habits:** You can tell when you're falling into old habits, shake yourself free, and move forward with intention and purpose.
- **Goals:** You understand how to set goals for yourself so that you don't have to flounder aimlessly anymore.

Don't be dismissive of how much information and mindset-shifting this is. This mental shit is exhausting on a good day.

I'm the first person to say how much I hate life transitions where I'm learning a bunch of super amazing shit. It's tiring, and painful, and I kinda just want it to be over. But what I've learned over time is that the hard parts in the middle of all that growth are worth the outcomes, because I come out closer and closer to exactly the person I want to be each time.

I hope you feel the same.

WHAT YOU'VE LEARNED ABOUT YOUR RELATIONSHIP WITH YOUR HOME

Kitchen, bedrooms, bathrooms, common spaces, clothes, storage, and sentimental crap: you've addressed it all.

To maintain your home in the state you want it, you'll have to stay on top of the new systems you've created for all of these areas. Realistic enough systems will almost feel like the spaces are maintaining themselves, because it will be so easy to do.

But even in the most organized home, you still have to pay attention. Life happens, and it gets messy.

The best-laid plans will get waylaid by things like illness, busy work, and school schedules, vacations, pets, and children. Trust me, I've had it happen way too many times in my own life to pretend it doesn't happen.

You're going along just fine, and then you get bitch-slapped by the universe, and you have to sit back for a bit while you regain your balance.

I once had a great plan and was going to take action into a whole new stage when I got waylaid first by a mystery gastric ailment that sidelined me for weeks, followed immediately by the flu, followed immediately by a freaking seizure. Yeah, a seizure. What the actual fuck!?

I had a choice: I could curl up into a ball and feel really sorry for myself while my house, my business, and my life crumbled around me, or I could take a few deep breaths and adjust the game plan. My ego didn't like it one bit, but I've found that letting my ego make the decisions isn't usually a good idea.

So, I adjusted.

My home got back on track. I adjusted my priorities for my health, which meant adjusting my boundaries with work, and I deep-breathed a ton of acceptance. The really fucked up part is that I needed to do all of those things anyways, so maybe the universe only bitch-slaps you when it knows you need it.

You'll adjust, too, when you need to. Trust in yourself.

KISS (KEEP IT SIMPLE, STUPID)

The last thing I want to leave you with is my favorite life rule for sustainability. Keep It Simple, Stupid. The KISS rule. A term that, fun fact, was originally coined by the US Navy in the 1960s.

Maintaining your home or your life can get out of control when it's overly complicated. Simplify whenever possible.

Simple is all about not overthinking things. If you catch yourself thinking too long and hard about something, you've probably swung past the solution and into outer space already.

Dial it back. Take yourself back to basics. Breathe.

Slow. The. Fuck. Down.

This isn't as complicated as you're making it. Quiet down the external noise, all the judgments, shoulds, and obligations. Tap into your intuition, your inner wisdom. Trust yourself. Don't trust yourself yet? Fake it until you get the evidence that you can in fact be trusted.

Decluttering your life and home is all about simplifying—having what you truly need, not what you think you're supposed to need.

Having what you love, not what you think you're supposed to love. Letting go of the need to judge and criticize yourself. Taking ownership of who you are, not who you think other people think you're supposed to be.

This is your life. This is your home. Own it.

MAKING IT REAL

At the beginning of this book, I promised you that you'd get to revisit the questions you answered in the Introduction by the time you got here. You've done a lot of work, and I know it's been tiring and hard at times, but I also hope it's been worth it. Keep in mind that you're not looking to move the needle from zero to 100: you're looking for evidence that something has shifted as you've thought about yourself and as you've worked on your home.

On a scale from 1–10 (1 being zilch and 10 being fully enlightened), how self-aware do you feel you are now? (Circle your number) **1** **2** **3** **4** **5** **6** **7** **8** **9** **10**	What tells you that's how self-aware you are? **For example:** *I still have no idea who I am,* **OR** *I'm totally noticing more often what my feelings are when they're happening.*
How often do you shit-talk yourself these days? (Circle one) **NEVER** **ONCE IN A WHILE** **ALL THE TIME**	What do you feel the reason is for this level of shit-talking? **For example:** *It just isn't something I'll ever be able to control,* **OR** *I'm learning to be more positive about myself and my life.*

You set three goals for yourself at the beginning of this book. How much progress have you made toward each of those goals? **1.** **2.** **3.**	You set three goals for your home at the beginning of this book. How much progress have you made toward each of those goals? **1.** **2.** **3.**	You set three additional goals at the beginning of this book. How much progress have you made toward each of those goals? **1.** **2.** **3.**
If you've completed the goals you set for yourself, what are three more you'd like to focus on? **1.** **2.** **3.**	If you've completed the goals you set for your home, what are three more you'd like to focus on? **1.** **2.** **3.**	If you've completed the additional goals you set, what are three more you'd like to focus on? **1.** **2.** **3.**

What have you changed to overcome the barriers to having a life you love?	What have you changed to overcome the barriers to having a home you love?	What are three MORE awesome things you know to be true about yourself? **1.** **2.** **3.**
What did you enjoy about decluttering the most?	Was the thing you were dreading about decluttering as awful as you expected it to be?	At the beginning, you said what you expected to get out of this book. What actually happened?

You've answered these three questions in each chapter of Part 2 for those areas. Now that you've decluttered your home (yay!), answer them while thinking about your home as a whole.
How do you feel when you think about your home now?
What new habits will you be putting in place to maintain your home?
Do you have any new goals for your home since decluttering?
BONUS: What do you need in order to increase your confidence that you can meet those new goals?

ABOUT THE AUTHOR

KATE EVANS is a psychologist and life coach with a Bachelor of Fine Arts from The University of Michigan, and a Master's in Professional Counseling from Argosy University. She decluttered her own home in 2018 and, having seen the connection to self-care, immediately began implementing decluttering in her work with clients. The joyful results led to writing the book *Ditch Your Sh*t*! Kate maintains her decluttered life with daily routines and yoga, and lives with her husband and two calico cats, none of whom will allow her to psychoanalyze them or declutter their toys.